'Adrian Webster is a real life example ‌‌‌‌‌‌‌‌‌‌‌‌‌‌‌‌‌‌‌‌‌ ...s all about.
I first travelled to London to see Adrian speak at an external conference having just read his book. I was blown away by his energy, emotion and delivery of what is a fantastic outlook on how to become successful in today's complicated social and economic world. Since then, Adrian has delivered three outstanding workshops and each time, my teams have gone on to deliver breakthrough performances. What sets Adrian apart is his energy, pace and passion in bringing to life the genuine accounts of his own road to Fat City. I defy anyone to attend a workshop of Adrian's and not be emotionally moved and motivated to start their Quest!'
– Martin C Bowmer
UK Head of Sales, Business Banking, Insurance and Investments, HSBC Bank Plc

'Adrian spoke at our company conference in 2005 and 2010 (outstanding). I recently found my 19 year old son John Pattison (just started a marketing job he seems to love) furtively reading *Polar Bear Pirates*. The next morning I found a note written by him to him before work – "FAT CITY HERE I COME". Thanks Adrian from two generations of Pattison's.'
– Paula Pattison
Senior Commercial Manager UK & Ireland, Hertel UK Ltd

'Everyone here is still buzzing ever since Adrian spoke at our conference, we are now completely focused on getting those TNTs right and inspired more than ever to continue making a very real difference to the lives of others.'
– Meenakshi Sharma
Change Manager, Merlin Housing Society

Adrian Webster

Polar Bear Pirates

and their quest to engage the sleepwalkers

Motivate Everyday People To
Deliver Extraordinary Results

Illustrations by Phil Williams

CAPSTONE

This edition first published by Capstone Publishing Ltd (a Wiley company), 2011
© 2011 Adrian Webster

Registered office
Capstone Publishing Ltd. (A Wiley Company), The Atrium, Southern Gate,
Chichester, West Sussex, PO19 8SQ, United Kingdom

For details of our global editorial offices, for customer services and for
information about how to apply for permission to reuse the copyright material in
this book please see our website at www.wiley.com.

Wiley also publishes its books in a variety of electronic formats. Some content
that appears in print may not be available in electronic books.

Designations used by companies to distinguish their products are often claimed
as trademarks. All brand names and product names used in this book are
trade names, service marks, trademarks or registered trademarks of their
respective owners. The publisher is not associated with any product or vendor
mentioned in this book. This publication is designed to provide accurate and
authoritative information in regard to the subject matter covered. It is sold on
the understanding that the publisher is not engaged in rendering professional
services. If professional advice or other expert assistance is required, the
services of a competent professional should be sought.

Library of Congress Cataloguing-in-Publication Data

9780857081278 (paperback), ISBN 9780857081629 (epub),
ISBN 9780857081636 (emobi), ISBN 9780857082398 (ebk)

A catalogue record for this book is available from the British Library.

Set in 9.5/14.5 pt Helvetica Neue by Toppan Best-set Premedia Limited

This book is dedicated to all those who every day climb their own mountains to help others.

I would like to thank Louise, Seb, Harry and Rosie without whom none of this would have been necessary!

My thanks also to Richard for waking me, Phil for his wonderful creativity, the Capstone Wiley team for all their fantastic support and James, Gordon, Jill, Mark, Dave and Hendo for continuing to be such good travelling companions.

In memory of my brother Stuart Webster.

Contents

INTRODUCTION – 1

WHO ARE THE SLEEPWALKERS? – 9

STEPPING BEYOND ORDINARY – 17

THE BEAUTIFUL PLANET COMPLACENCY – 27

GROWING PEOPLE IN A FAMILY ENVIRONMENT – 31

LOOK SIDEWAYS AS WELL AS VERTICALLY – 41

AMPS AND VAMPS – 49

THE SPERM THAT WON – 59

TNT STICKY PICTURE BOMBS – HANDLE WITH CARE! – 69

WHY WAKE UP FOR YOU? – 89

DON'T DO PERFECT – 101

SONAR LEADERS – 109

DEVELOPING THEIR PICTURES TOGETHER – 119

MAKING TIME AND SPACE FOR THE BIG
DOABLE STUFF – 125

YOUR GROUND RULES – 135

THE POWER OF PEERS – 143

GET OUT OF THAT BOX! – 149

THE DENT YOU LEAVE BEHIND – 155

HEALTH WARNING – 161

SIX POLAR BEAR PIRATE ATTITUDES FOR THE
JOURNEY AHEAD – 165

POLAR BEAR PIRATE TERMINOLOGY – 167

ABOUT ADRIAN WEBSTER – 173

Introduction

Fat City is where the winners live. Most people who live there came from Rock Bottom. No one has ever moved there from Complacency, that's where The Norms live. To get there, you carry on doing what you've always done.

My first book was very much about self motivation and finding true success, what Polar Bear Pirates call Fat City. It was also about combating a range of negative characters in the workplace that we all come across on the road to Fat City, no doubt you'll probably recognise a few of them:

Neg Ferrets are little warriors of doom who spend their lives macheteing their way through all things positive to find just one little negative. They're like little indoor rain clouds, they have a problem for every solution and light up the room when they walk out.

Bloaters are Boasting, Lazy, Obnoxious And Tediously Egotistical, Reptilian Saddos. They have degrees in hindsight, they possess the answers to the universe and have an opinion on absolutely everything. Whatever you've done, they've done it, but much bigger and better than you. You name it, they've got the T-shirt.

Sinkers are disciples of your pear shape who are desperate to pull as many people down as possible into the boat of failure where they reside. Having never really achieved anything themselves, they despise other people's success and will do their very best to torpedo anyone else's attempts at reaching Fat City.

Head Treads are the most insecure of all enemies. They live on the outskirts of Fat City having only just made it there through brown nosing, knife throwing, toadying and luck. Terrified of anyone coming along with real talent, they are the ladder pullers of Fat City.

Given half a chance, all of these enemies of success will do their utmost to slow, hinder, block or puncture your progress along the road to your Fat City. To avoid repetition for those who have read my first book, I will collectively refer to them in this book as 'The Pothole People' – they are best avoided!

In their fight against negativity Polar Bear Pirates have a very loyal ally. Betty Backroom is the dedicated, behind the scenes, limelight shunning, unsung linchpin heroine of any great team. The Bettys of this world are the keepers of sanity who get things done, they hold their teams together, keep the ship on course and manage their boss.

Don't mess with Betty B!

There is however a much greater and far deadlier enemy out there. A most deceptive enemy that today, more than ever, poses a substantially graver threat to those travelling on the road to Fat City than all of the Pothole People put together. As far as Polar Bear Pirates are concerned Planet Complacency is public enemy number one.

This book is all about engaging and inspiring others to keep moving on together as far away from Planet Complacency as possible, to fight its seductive powers and one day reach Fat City. It's about getting the very best out of everyday people and motivating them to want to get out of bed, to come into work and deliver extraordinary results. It's about creating an environment that encourages people to grow and it's about helping them to realise that they make a difference, no matter what role they play.

It's also very much about re-engaging characters that we all come across or find ourselves working alongside. I'm talking about The Sleepwalkers.

So who are the Polar Bear Pirates? From all walks of life, they are believers in life before death who just get on with it and really make a difference. They are everyday people who deliver extraordinary results, day in, day out.

On the surface they tend to have a warm, fun loving and at times, cuddly appearance. Scratch that surface and you will find a rather unique, highly focused individual that is prepared to do what most others aren't – to take that extra step, beyond the ordinary.

Their success is very much down to two things, firstly their ability to embrace change and move on and secondly their attitude towards problems. They regard problems as being pregnant with opportunity.

As team players, Polar Bear Pirates also have something else in common; they have such an abundance of talent and self-belief in their own abilities that they are more than happy to share their knowledge, energy and experience with others.

Above all else, they relish challenges and there is no bigger challenge as far as they are concerned than trying to inspire others with far less belief than themselves, to join them on their journey to Fat City.

Who are The Sleepwalkers?

Although at the time we were probably unaware of it, many of us have at some stage in our careers been a Sleepwalker. They are those who are loaded with potential, but who without even realising it, have gradually become passively disengaged. Having carried on doing what they've always done, they've unwittingly ended up becoming trapped, suspended in space, going around and around Planet Complacency.

Sleepwalkers do an adequate job but, as they proved in their first three months, they are capable of doing so much more. Having become too used to what they do, their lights are still on but they just don't shine like they used to, unbeknown to them their batteries have run low. Capable of delivering 100 watts, they only manage to give out 60, with the occasional dazzling flicker of their true potential on a good day.

They turn up for work and slip into their comfy routine, just doing enough by simply going through the motions, cruising the week with their eyes half open, looking forward to the weekend, doing what they've always done, thinking the same old stuff and delivering the same results.

Some will tell you they have five years' experience, when in reality they may only actually have one year's experience but have done the same thing five times.

They may be one hundred percent with you in body but as long as they continue to sleepwalk, they will be incapable of taking that extra step beyond ordinary. Blissfully unaware and drawn by its seductive gravitational pull they've drifted into the orbit of Planet Complacency where their minds have slipped into sleep mode.

To see Sleepwalkers in action you need look no further than people you most likely come across every day of the week, that's because they tend to stand out like beacons of disappointment when they are in customer facing roles. I know this because just like most other people, I deal with companies over the phone, I experience the deep joy of going shopping and quite often, I stay in hotels.

I'll get a fabulous, glossy hotel brochure arrive in the post assuring me of the warmest welcome I'll have ever experienced. The centre fold pages of this wonderfully crafted, awe inspiring corporate masterpiece are dedicated to a picture of a positively glowing receptionist greeting travellers just like me. My expectations are raised to such a level, that the air feels thin.

The booking made, and off I head to experience my warm welcome. Seven hours and countless sets of road works later I eventually arrive at my destination, a palatial oasis. The building, with its pink marble flooring is, just as the brochure describes it, 'quite magnificent'. Yes, the building may be magnificent but who have they employed behind reception the day I turn up? The friendly, glowing face in my brochure?

No! It must be their day off, because the day I arrive they've got someone 'greeting me' who has the same warmth and charisma as my sat nav.

Just like so many of the shop assistants I come across, they appear to be in cruise control, simply going through the motions and just doing enough. Even in some cases when they are actually using words like 'please' and 'thank you' and on the odd leap year occasion not only using these words but also smiling, all at the same time. There isn't anything that I can put my finger on or if I wanted to, complain about, they've done nothing wrong.

Yet, despite them doing and saying all the right things, it still feels like I'm not being served but merely 'dealt with' by either some sort of roboserve android or someone who is living in a parallel universe.

Why? Because there is no warm feeling, no emotion, no connection, no energy, that little extra something is missing.

The truth is, they may be stood right in front of me, breathing, walking, perspiring and alas, on some occasions giving me the distinct impression that they don't floss too often. However, despite all the physical evidence standing or sitting before me, something tells me that they're not really here with me on this planet right now. Their minds seem to be elsewhere, I don't know where. I can only assume that they must be sleepwalking.

Sleepwalkers however are not just confined to customer facing roles! It's just that these are the tips of the icebergs of mediocre performance. These are the ones that we notice because we are looking through the more focused eyes of a paying customer. Behind every one that we as customers come across, there are countless millions of others out there, working in very different roles and on every rung of every ladder.

They can be found in big, medium, small and one man band organisations. From manual workers to CEOs, right across the private and public sectors. In every nook and cranny, throughout all the professions, behind every door on every floor. On trains, planes, buses and bicycles, in colleges, hospitals, factories, on our streets, in the skies, on waterways, up and down motorways and on our undergrounds. This Sleepwalking epidemic is sweeping across the world, leaving no area of the workplace untouched, chances are there's a Sleepwalker sat or standing next to you right now.

If you are looking for one near you, the most obvious symptom is an apparent reluctance to get involved in anything outside of their immediate job spec.

They appear on the surface to embrace change and fresh ideas but in truth they lean back and simply 'ride out' any new initiatives, allowing them to fizzle out and die, just like all the others that have passed them by. They stand back and watch others muck in and carry the rest of the team.

They welcome new enthusiastic managers, assuring them of their support whilst at the same time hoping deep down that they too will run out of steam. At meetings they sit back, avoiding any responsibility and suddenly become limbo dance champions, sliding down their seats and trying to hide under the table when it comes to the 'who's going to action what' bit.

So why have these once enthusiastic tail waggers who first joined your team become like this? Why are they in sleep mode or should I say standby mode? The reason for this Sleepwalking epidemic is not purely down to each individual concerned, although they must share some responsibility, it's also very much down to the people around them, and in particular their managers for allowing these good people to become disengaged.

If only these managers could themselves wake up, lift their heads up, take a good look around and see just how much dormant talent they have in their teams. If only they would realise just how much more these Sleepwalkers have to offer and how much more could be achieved.

If they could just wake them, re-engage, and inspire them to once again lean in and move on. If they could perhaps entice them to want to join them on their journey and re-energise them enough to pull away from Planet Complacency and take that extra step beyond ordinary.

Stepping Beyond ordinary

The difference between ordinary and extraordinary is the tiniest of steps but it's that crucial step that differentiates and defines individuals and teams.

If as a leader you can encourage most of your people to take this step beyond ordinary you are doing really well. If however you can inspire all of your people to take this extra step together as one team, well that's when something really special happens, the norm line shifts and what was once regarded as extraordinary, becomes ordinary.

This tiny step, if taken by everyone all at the same time, will open up a narrow gap between you and your competition, a slender gap that's of light year significance, propelling you as a team out into the fast lane and leaving them behind in the bus lane.

In sport, this step is often less than a thousandth of a second, it's one point, one shot, one goal, one inch, one miss, one slip. It's the cruel heart beat difference between winning and losing, it's the difference between someone being a good club player and someone competing at the highest level. It's the difference between silver and gold and it's the difference between a collection of individuals and a high performance winning team.

In the workplace, it's the difference between people doing a good job and people making a difference.

If fire fighting managers are to step into the shoes of leaders and inspire their people to deliver world class results, and if they are to ensure that their teams differentiate themselves from their competitors, they will need as many people as possible, especially themselves, taking this vital step.

I spent most of my career working in target driven environments; it always seemed like tough times because we always had massive targets to meet. We were always up against fierce competition and on top of all that, we always had head hunters trying to snatch any good staff we had.

The one thing that I never ever had as a manager was the luxury of a big budget and I certainly didn't have the money that many of our bigger competitors appeared to have. When I think about it, the only real resource I had around me in my teams was people like me, everyday people. Together as everyday people we had to pull together as one big team, we had to put customers at the heart of everything we did and constantly look at ourselves through their eyes. We also had to do something else, we had to differentiate ourselves on a day to day basis from our competition.

As a result, to try and motivate people I had to move away from being a fire fighting manager and try to step into the shoes of a leader. I had to come up with something different, something that would help inspire and engage everyday people around me to deliver extraordinary results – the world of Polar Bear Pirates was born.

Let me ask you a question. When you left school, did you set out to do exactly the role that you've ended up doing now?

I'm making a calculated guess here that your answer to this question is more likely to be a 'no' than a 'yes'. The reason for me being fairly sure of this, although I could be wrong, is that in the past twelve months I've posed this exact same question to each of the very different audiences at events that I've been fortunate enough to speak at. In total, out of approximately a hundred conferences, only about twenty or so people have put their hands up and answered 'yes'.

You see most people don't end up doing what they originally set out to do, I certainly didn't, but I somehow had to try and motivate myself and others around me in an environment that for the vast majority of us, wasn't our very first choice.

Without intending to sound cynical here, I've always been able to understand people finding the inspiration to climb mountains, to sail oceans or even trek to The South Pole.

If you and I had to meet up tomorrow morning at the airport at 4am because we were setting off on a polar expedition, we'd both be pretty buzzed up, even at that time in the morning. Don't get me wrong, people climbing mountains and trekking to the Poles is, without doubt highly inspirational stuff and it certainly makes great television viewing, but I can easily see where the motivation is coming from.

But what motivates the rest of us? What motivates everyday people in the real world to want to get out of bed each day and in their own way climb their own mountains and make a difference in their workplace?

'What motivates everyday people in the real world to want to get out of bed each day and

in their own way climb their own mountains and make a difference in their workplace?'

What motivates a postman or a post lady on a relatively low income not only to just do their bit and deliver the post, but to want to step beyond their job spec five or six days a week and put some smiles on a few recipients' faces? It's certainly not just for the money.

What motivates someone driving a forklift truck, right now, working in some dark damp warehouse just down the road from you to want to bother putting all the pallets in exactly the right place, especially when their supervisor isn't around?

What motivates a receptionist or a managing director? What motivates someone in HR, Sales, I.T, Finance, Marketing, Operations, Payroll, Engineering, Consultancy, Admin, Support, Customer Services, Accounts, Despatch? What motivates a nurse, a chef, a paramedic, a housing officer, a surveyor, a carpenter, a middle manager, a caretaker, a cleaner or any self employed person? What motivates anyone in their workplace to want to take that extra tiny step and really make a difference?

The saddest people of all for me are the people I call the 'I'm Justs'. Almost every time I'm lucky enough to get shown around an organisation, I come across 'I'm Justs'.

When I meet them I feel like I'm going to self combust with a mixture of sadness for them and anger with their management. I want to pick them and their managers up and shake them!

You see, you meet such fantastic, loyal, hard working people but, on asking them in all seriousness what they do as part of their team, they respond by looking down at the floor and sheepishly beginning their answer with 'I'm just'. 'I'm just in I.T', 'I'm just in training', 'I'm just in sales', 'I'm just in HR', 'I'm just in . . .'

I was once being shown around a fabulous educational establishment when I met a lovely lady who responded with 'I'm just a teacher'. Argh!

Who on earth should ever regard themselves as an I'm Just? How can anyone have any self pride or any dignity, let alone come out of sleep mode and begin to make a difference if they seriously regard themselves as an 'I'm just'?

My father who died in 2006 at the age of eighty-eight was once a Yorkshire coal miner and if you'd said to him, 'Apparently Jack Webster, you were once just a coal miner.' He'd probably have just about found enough strength left in his body to try and get out of his chair to look you straight in the eyes and point out that he wasn't just a coal miner – he was a very good coal miner!

He was ferociously proud of the fact that he'd been a miner. Apparently they shifted more tonnage of coal from his pit than any other pit in the area and, according to Dad, a lot of good men, far better men than him as he described them, had lost their lives doing it.

If we were to stop teenagers on the streets right now, anywhere in the world and ask them what in their heart of hearts, deep down they'd really love to be when they leave school, in this celebrity driven, 'X Factor' era we live in, a lot of them if they were being completely honest with us would probably turn round and tell us that they would love to be rock stars, pop stars, movie stars, sports stars and even catwalk stars.

I wish them all the best and I hope that they do indeed achieve their dream and end up as a megastar. However, without wishing to sneeze in their popcorn, the truth is that there are billions of applicants out there for every one megastar vacancy.

Does it not mean though that if they don't achieve their first choice, dream role in life, they cannot come into your workplace and under your guidance and leadership, with a few good team mates around them, end up feeling like a bit of a star, no matter whatever they end up doing?

My eyes had been opened to true stardom at the age of nineteen, when I first joined the police. Having attended the scenes of a couple of particularly bad road traffic accidents I witnessed some real stars in action. Ambulance drivers, police officers, fire crews, doctors and nurses, I don't think any of them were ever asked for their autograph but all of them were indeed superstars, just getting on with it, climbing mountains to help others and making an immeasurable difference.

One Monday evening I went to visit my Grandma in hospital. Having spent a good hour or so chatting with her, the doors to the ward slowly creaked open. From them emerged a tea trolley. Following on behind it was a lady whom I can only describe as the most miserable looking human being I had ever seen. Plucking up courage, I went up to her and politely asked if I could possibly have a cup of tea or coffee. Without even looking at me, she growled in a voice that sounded like something out of the morgue 'patients only', and that was the end of that brief but memorable encounter.

Four evenings later I returned to visit Grandma. Suddenly the doors to the ward once again slowly began to open and the very same tea trolley reappeared. This time however it was being pushed along by a rather large and very jolly looking, middle aged West Indian lady. She parked the trolley to one side and with a huge infectious smile on her face, she announced her arrival by bellowing down the ward with considerable enthusiasm, 'Good evening ladies and gentlemen, who would like a cup of tea?!'

This wonderful, megastar lady literally lit the place up, the weather in the ward instantly changed and even those who just moments earlier had looked like they were at death's door had smiles on their faces.

When she arrived at Grandma's bed, I asked her if I could have a cup of tea and she replied with a glint in her eye: 'Of course you can, but let's serve the lady first!'

Yes, it was the same trolley, the same ward, the same working conditions and probably exactly the same hours and money for both these two ladies. So why was one just doing the bare minimum and the other taking so much pride in her job, stepping beyond her job spec, being a superstar tea lady, feeling good about herself and making such a difference?

Many years later, when I first started managing teams of people, I noticed that out of say a hundred people there would be just a very small handful of people who I would class as superstar performers.

I was intrigued and at the same time I desperately needed everyone in my teams to deliver results, so I set about finding out what makes certain everyday people so successful.

Twenty years later and I still haven't discovered a single secret to success! In fact I don't think anybody has any secrets to success, anyone who claims they have, has got to be full of manure.

I don't think there are any secrets but I do think there are a few very important keys, none of which I'm pleased to report are ever likely to be classified as rocket science.

The Beautiful Planet complacency

Wen it comes to preventing people from reaching their Fat City, there is no bigger or deadlier enemy out there. Planet Complacency is the arch enemy of success. Holding back people from taking that extra step beyond ordinary, it has been responsible over the years for snuffing out millions of people's dreams, kidnapping untold potential and murdering in their infancy what would have gone on to be countless extraordinary achievements.

'Planet Complacency is the arch enemy of success.'

This huge planet has not only the most powerful but also by far the most deceptive gravitational pulls of all places, far more so than that of Rock Bottom. The reason being is that unlike the dark, lonely and so obviously inhospitable place that is Rock Bottom, which as soon as anyone claps eyes on it, they want to spin on their heels and run as far away as possible from it. Planet Complacency in complete contrast appears to be such a comfortable, safe, warm, welcoming and popular place to be.

Over the years this silent assassin has claimed more victims than all the other enemies along the road to Fat City put together, drawing in entire teams, lulling them into a false sense of security, inducing sleep mode and holding them completely unaware, suspended in its honey trap orbit.

Its hypnotic pull is so easy to give in to. Even the most determined, high flying people have been seduced by its beauty. Having slowed down for just one moment, they have fallen for its mesmeric charms and ended up being sucked into its orbit. Drifting around and around and going nowhere. It's just so easy for people to lean back, go with the flow, have a little nap and let someone else do the driving.

It will only be when you try to wake them and pull them away that as a leader you'll discover the true force of Planet Complacency's formidable appeal. Fighting its gravitational pull and snatching people away from its grasp is hard but it's certainly not impossible. It can only be achieved if you and all your people pull together as one big team and use your biggest team weapon of all to fight it, your combined energy.

It is imperative that if you are to avoid Planet Complacency you do two things: Stay focused at all times and keep on going forwards!

Growing People In A Family Environment

f I am to get the very best out of everyone around me, keep them away from the deadly reaches of Planet Complacency and help them deliver extraordinary results, the first thing I will need to do is to create an environment that not only keeps people wide awake, but at the same time encourages and enables them to grow.

To do this I will need to go beyond building a team and create a close knit sharing family unit that's based on trust. I want to develop a family winning environment within which everyone has a buy in, takes ownership, looks forward to coming into work and wants to take that extra step.

If people are going continue to progress, and one day witness with their own eyes their own true potential, I will need to keep them engaged and at the same time challenged. As well as all this, if I am to hatch out some real success and germinate a few seeds of innovative thinking around the place, I must have three things; light, warmth and a very small widget of fear.

Have you ever noticed in warm sunny climates the size of some of the plants? In comparison with their puny, stunted cousins that can be found withering away in the cold corners of this planet, these light seeking, heat loving giants are positively thriving.

The difference between the two is the environment that they are in. Both kinds may have ample water, oxygen and their fair share of light but only one kind has both light and warmth, and that's the big ones.

People are exactly the same and if I am going to have a winning team I'll need to grow some pretty big people around me. We as a team are going to have to constantly produce enough in house energy to provide both light and warmth to keep us all together, moving on in the right direction and ahead of the competition.

When I'm talking about light in the workplace I'm talking about having an open, transparent environment. An environment that provides people with clarity so that everyone understands what is expected of them and can see where they are heading. An environment where everyone is focused on and working together towards common goals. Like plants, people will always grow towards the light. Yes, the old analogy about keeping people in the dark and ending up with mushrooms really is true.

When I'm talking about warmth in the workplace I'm talking about people feeling cared for, trusted, supported, protected, sharing, having some fun and having the warm glow of recognition pointed in their direction now and then.

I've seen some brightly lit, great looking sunny workplace environments where company visions are displayed on walls, career paths are mapped out, everyone has clear direction, goals are all highly visible and the rewards for success are generous. But, people still aren't growing like they should be because despite all the light, all the sunshine, their environment lacks warmth.

Sunshine doesn't necessarily mean warmth. Something some people should perhaps bear in mind if ever they do start looking around for another job.

I honestly believe that some managers genuinely think that good leadership is simply about setting clear objectives for their team. That it's about dishing out precise instructions chiselled out in stone and then 'ordering' them to get on with it.

Well that'll be it, piece of cake! They'll be able to sit back in their offices, fiddling with the height adjusters on their chairs and pop by Planet Complacency whilst they wait for the glory from the toils of their team to come seeping under their firmly closed office doors.

On the other hand, I've seen people surrounded by warmth that's been given off by caring, well intentioned, passionate managers. But their people never grow because there's not enough light! They maybe very well supported, cared for, nurtured, loved to bits and having great fun, but with their managers sending out smoke signals in the fog they have no direction and nothing to focus on. They don't have a clue as to where they're heading and instead of clarity they are surrounded by what can best be described as cluttered confusion, created by their well meaning, lovable but rudderless managers.

Part of creating warmth is having some fun. Fun is so important but often forgotten, completely misunderstood or mistaken for being unprofessional and rather silly. Fun is in fact a highly productive, completely free cost saving thing because when people are having fun, endorphins are released which make people feel relaxed and happy. When people are relaxed and happy they are able to be themselves, forget their worries, work together and perform at their best. Amazingly enough, results go up and sick days go down.

'When people are relaxed and happy they are able to be themselves, forget their worries, work together and perform at their best.'

I'm highlighting fun here because some senior people do look at me with a very worried look on their face when having asked me what they could do to improve the working environment for their people I suggest, amongst other things, to help make it a warmer place they could try making it a bit more fun. I think when they imagine people having fun they must think of them just messing about wasting their time and money or perhaps even picturing their staff wearing red noses, answering the phone with helium voices, making paper aeroplanes, popping party poppers and doing the conga around the office.

When I picture people having fun in the workplace I picture people working hard with smiles on their faces, getting stuck in together, getting a real buzz from being busy and having a few good laughs. It's an old one but a favourite saying amongst Polar Bear Pirates 'When things are fun, work gets done'.

If I am going to grow really big people and get them to step beyond ordinary as well as the essential elements of light and warmth, I will need to keep them stimulated through continuously setting them new challenges. This will mean gradually bringing into play a little helper in the back of their minds to give them a little boost and help them to achieve these challenges. A tiny home grown widget of fear which to help you picture it, if it was an actual physical thing, would not be a million miles dissimilar to those you find at the bottom of some beer cans to help build up a small amount of pressure upon opening.

In my opinion the two most basic motivators out there are the positive one, love and the negative one, fear. People will either be inspired to do something because they'd love to do it or because they fear not doing it.

I'll give you a simple example of the motivating effects of fear. If you were being chased by a great white shark, the thought of not getting away from it would probably inspire you to not only break all Olympic swimming records but at the very same time to become the first known person ever to run a hundred metres in under nine seconds, on water. I say known person because I dare say down through the centuries there are quite a few people who having been pursued by sharks, crocs and other such beasties have actually achieved this incredible feat but obviously weren't around long enough to claim the record.

Fear is indeed a phenomenal stimulant but unfortunately out of the two, love and fear, fear is by far the most popular choice of weak managers. A lot of insecure bullying managers were abused by their self styled Sergeant Shout manager and as a result of being put through the mill they want to dish out what they had doled out to them and put as many people as possible through the very same mill.

It's so much easier to make people fear things, including themselves, than it is to get them to love them. However, when too much fear is applied people become disengaged and act like frightened hedgehogs, they tighten up into defensive spiky balls and you get nothing out of them. To really get people pushing themselves to take that extra step I would much prefer them to do it for positive reasons, in other words because they want to.

As a leader the only drop of fear I ever want anyone in my teams to ever have, is a tiny amount of self produced organic fear in the back of their own minds of letting themselves and the rest of their team down.

From a combination of these two things that little widget of fear should come into play when a new challenge or opportunity opens up before them, activating the widget and instantly inducing a healthy build up of pressure to a level that's just enough to give them a gentle nudge and help them perform at their very best.

It will only work if they really do want to succeed at whatever it is they are trying to achieve and at the same time they care about and respect those around them. It is therefore essential that if I want them to have this drop of built in fear, I as their leader focus purely on the positive motivators by:

(a)   Inspiring them to want to take that next step.

(b)   Building a close knit winning family around them.

The more successful I am at developing these two areas, the more chance I will have of continuing to detonate a few widgets around the place and help my people to continue to step together beyond Planet Complacency.

I would never ever dream of openly using fear as some sort of motivational stick or of even pointing it out to anyone. I don't need to and besides that, pointing out fear never works. Fear of letting themselves or others down has to come from within them and them only. Not coming from within an individual but from an external source especially their manager will simply come across for what it is: emotional blackmail. And anyway, if you start mentioning widgets in people's heads they'll think you really have gone fruit loops!

With good leadership skills, the right people around them and the right environment, their own fear of not giving it their very best shot will thankfully be the only kind of fear that they will ever need to reach Fat City.

How your people grow and what they will eventually become will very much be determined by the environment that you create around them.

Look Sideways As Well As Vertically

I f your people regard success purely as going up and up a ladder and everybody wants their boss's job, you'll end with a weak and unhappy team.

It's important that people also see success as growing themselves sideways in their roles as well as progressing upwards. Enjoying what they do, priding themselves on being the best they can be, using their talents, making a difference, feeling validated and receiving some much deserved peer recognition now and again for what they bring to the table, should be what true success is all about.

As mentioned earlier, people will always grow towards the light so if we are to grow people sideways as well as upwards we have to make sure that the only light they are seeing isn't just the one from above. There should be encouragement for them to develop in whatever direction they feel happiest and best equipped to go in.

Just because someone isn't chasing promotion doesn't mean they should be regarded as being any less ambitious than someone who is. Their ambition might be to become the very best they can possibly be and stay in the role that they currently do. If a teacher doesn't aspire to be a head teacher, but wants to stay in their current position in the same school and for their entire career, that doesn't mean that they're not motivated. Nor does it mean that they have entered the orbit of Planet Complacency. Far from it, it may be that their picture of Fat City is to be a great teacher and continue to be so at the same school.

Success is all about the attitude we have towards it, how we perceive it and how we feel within ourselves. I've always measured success not by the job title that someone has or the car they drive but by how much of a difference they make.

I'm a motivational business speaker, I absolutely love what I do and I wouldn't want to do anything else. Now this doesn't mean I'm not ambitious, I most certainly am, my ambition is to continuously improve, to grow as a speaker and be able to make as big a difference as possible.

People should be able to feel that they are still achieving and being highly successful by doing what they do extremely well and not necessarily having to gain promotion to feel or be regarded by others as being successful.

'People should be able to feel that they are still achieving and being highly successful by doing what they do extremely well and not necessarily having to gain promotion to feel or be regarded by others as being successful.'

It was brought home to me that the way success is viewed and quantified by the most successful teams is one of the most important keys to their success. It happened several years ago when I stumbled across a shining example of someone who had obviously grown themselves within their role and taken full ownership of it.

It was when I first ever stayed at Gleneagles in Scotland for a conference I was speaking at. At breakfast I asked the head of training how the lady on reception the previous evening had remembered my name from checking me in several hours earlier, knew it was my first ever stay there and remembered what time I was booked into the restaurant for dinner.

He replied 'Adrian, she is a professional receptionist'.

I thought 'wow!' What a great attitude. No wonder they're so stunningly good at what they do as a team.

The last time I had to pop down to my local post office depot in Maidstone to collect a parcel, based on past experiences I wasn't exactly expecting to be blown away by what you'd call a terrific customer service experience. Despite the excitement of looking forward to discovering what the contents of my mystery package might be, memories of my last visit weren't particularly pleasant ones. I could remember a fairly drab, non descript office but what I could remember vividly was a fed up looking man standing behind the counter asking me for ID and scowling at me for daring to intrude into his world and interrupt the private conversation he was having with an out of sight colleague about not getting a long enough lunch break.

He reluctantly trudged off to go and look for my parcel and returned what seemed like hours later, handing it over to me with all the enthusiasm of a pallbearer.

On this visit however, things had dramatically changed beyond all recognition. The collection office was physically still exactly the same but something was new. I could instantly sense a very different atmosphere and the reason for this suddenly popped up from behind the counter in front of me. I was literally knocked back by the delightful person who suddenly emerged. Smiling and appearing just as excited as I was about how big the parcel I was just about to receive was going to be. She bounced off to look for it and emerged moments later having found it with a beaming expression of delight on her face. You would have thought that it was a surprise gift for her!

I was so taken aback by this charismatic person and her fantastic positive attitude that I asked her for her name. She said 'Everyone calls me Curls'. I asked her if she enjoyed her work and she replied 'I love it!'

At Bearsted train station just down the road from me there are two really successful people working there, Alan and Richard. Their role is to look after the station and its passengers, as well as give out train tickets. But, that's not all they do, not by a long shot, they have both grown much bigger than that. Even on the darkest and coldest of mornings they always have time for people, remembering their names, asking how they are, cheering travellers up and making a difference. I asked Alan why they both always seem to put so much into it. He said 'We both really enjoy what we do'.

The truth is they are probably a lot happier and as a result more successful in their work than the vast majority of commuters who board the trains there each morning.

Curls, Alan and Richard aren't working in the magnificent surroundings of Gleneagles but just like the professional receptionist there, they too are highly successful people. None of the above examples are Chief Executives, Board Directors or Senior Partners, they probably wouldn't want to be but they are all very big people who turn in a personal best every day.

They have grabbed hold of their roles by both hands, made them their own, developed them way beyond the margins of their job specs and continued to progress way beyond Planet Complacency towards Fat City.

It is important that your people are able to see some progress even if that progress is only slow progress. To regard themselves as being successful, they may not necessarily feel that they have to be heading upwards but they will all need to sense that they are getting somewhere. In particular, those who are seeking promotion will need to be challenged and stretched to the best of their abilities if you are to give them a sense of achievement and retain them, especially if there is a lack of openings above them. It's vital that people are recognised for what they do, that there are opportunities for them to develop within their existing roles and that they are able to feel that they are making a difference.

If you want people to grow they must feel good about themselves.

Amps And Vamps

Everyone is different, is motivated by different things and if you look closely enough has a gift to offer. However, in saying this, I have over the years noticed that both extraordinary people and highly successful teams all share one thing in common, they all appear to have an abundance of energy. So much so that in some cases, and I swear that I'm not imagining this, that just like when you walk past an electricity sub-station, you can actually detect a low but perfectly audible hum.

Some individuals seem to have such high energy levels that their energy can't be contained; it spills over and creates a magnetic field around them that attracts others. You can actually feel energy radiating around them and sense it sparking off them, jumping across to anyone who comes into contact with them, getting them all buzzed up too.

Energy levels play a huge part in just how well an individual or a team is going to perform. How energy is created, shared and harnessed is extremely important when it comes to team work and in particular, when we're trying to provide the right environment to grow people away from Planet Complacency.

When it comes to people and energy, there are definitely two distinct types, the Amps and the Vamps. The exothermic (give off heat) Amps generate most of their own positive energy most of the time. The endothermic (absorb heat) Vamps on the other hand need to constantly feed off the energy of those around them.

The Amps although at times they do still need re-energising, are your rock solid, dependable team treasures who are always there, dedicated and delivering. They are ferociously loyal allies of Polar Bear Pirates, and if you were to cut them in half you'd be sure to find their team name tattooed across their heart. Far more self motivated and more capable of working off their own backs than Vamps, they maintain consistent and constant, slow burn, positive energy levels that radiate light and warmth around the place.

Not all of them will set the world alight but when the chips are down they'll be the ones who if you look after them, will look after you and the rest of the team. Their pilot lights are always lit.

The Vamps however tend to be far more up and down and only work at their best when there is a constant external source of positive energy, readily available to them, on tap and close by. As individuals they are not necessarily negative characters, they're not Pothole People but they do need to lean on others for support.

Despite this, Vamps are in fact capable of becoming highly energised very quickly and delivering outstanding results. If that is, they have the right people around them, keeping them sparked up, supported and supplying them with the right kind of energy.

One of the drawbacks with Vamps, besides not being very good at energising themselves and keeping themselves up, is that they are pretty hopeless when it comes to maintaining their own energy levels especially when the going gets tough. They tend to demonstrate high levels of energy but only in short bursts. Left unengaged for just a short period of time, their energy levels can drop off sharply. Losing power, their batteries draining and no one around to give them a lift, they will slow down rapidly and quickly drift towards Planet Complacency.

The biggest problem with Vamps though is that in their need to feed off others they tend to suck up and absorb whatever energy happens to be around, whether it's positive or negative. In other words these energy sensitive, mood swing characters are easily influenced by whoever happens to be around and the environment they are in.

As a result, if they are left to their own devices with little support from the right people, it is not only highly likely that they will become Sleepwalkers, but much worse still, whilst in Sleepwalker mode, become top of the list, prime target recruitment candidates for those pedalling negative energy, The Pothole People.

One moment they'll be sat in front of you, listening with great excitement to your plans and the new one team vision and wanting to be very much part of it. Telling you how much they love their job and the opportunity that they now have to really shine, appearing to be all fired up and literally bursting at the seams with enthusiasm for what lies ahead.

A few hours later they'll be in a bar, soaking up the sulphurous atmosphere as they sit listening to and nodding in agreement with a group of Pothole People who are holding an offsite pre-mortem meeting into everything that they predict is going to go wrong.

As a leader you will need to keep an eye on them and be pre-pared to quickly re-ignite them when they are down. It would be a good idea to try and make sure where possible that they are in the company of the more consistent, slow burn Amps who can help keep them supported and supplied with the right brand of energy and prevent them turning Pothole.

Unfortunately there are a lot more Vamps around than there are Amps and Vamps do use up a lot more of the team energy than Amps. However, although exothermic, not all Amps are the same.

You have the closed Amp who is, for most of the time, self stoking but at the same time quite happily self contained. This type of more single minded Amp, although capable of working as part of a team and of giving off light and warmth for others, much prefers to be left alone, to be allowed to just get on with it, to deliver results and keep most of their home grown energy for their own use.

Then there is the open Amp. Although they are more than capable of working off their own backs and of achieving results for themselves, they are happiest, in their element and at their very best when sharing their abundant energy around the place for the greater good of the rest of the team.

Constantly giving out positive energy, these 'Hummers', as I call them, thrive on energising and developing others. They make great mentors, coaches and Betty Backrooms.

Due to their never fading positive attitude and their ability to get things done, Amps, whether open or closed, along with Polar Bear Pirates are the sworn enemies of The Pothole People.

The Pothole People have a pathological hatred of them. They despise and fear everything that they stand for, knowing full well that with Amps about their chances of derailing new initiatives, recruiting Sleepwalkers to their miserable hidden agendas and puncturing the wheels of progress will be greatly inhibited.

Yes, these ever dependable, unassuming team radiators are the energy grid gate keepers of all great teams and are almost as rare as rocking horse droppings. So, if you have an Amp in your team, look after them!

One of the keys to keeping positive energy levels charged up at all times and to keep your people motivated is to know your Amps from your Vamps and your closed Amps from your open Amps.

'Know your Amps from your Vamps and your closed Amps from your open Amps.'

Both open and closed Amps can, if utilised correctly, be a massive benefit to the team, not only providing energy for light and warmth, they gel the team together, keep it focused and in times of crisis keep things sane. You must however, if you want to get the very best out of your people have all your jigsaw pieces in the right places i.e. everyone in precisely the right roles.

A main cause of people underperforming is because they're not very happy in their role. More often than not if you change their role, adjust it or even in some instances just tweak it slightly it can have a massive effect. Suddenly they're performing again and they're like a changed person.

The key is to have a good balanced mix of Amps and Vamps and to get your corner pieces, your Amps, in position first so that they can look after, protect and help keep your Vamps positively fed.

The real trick, which any Polar Bear Pirate leader will tell you, is to let your open Amps drive the team forward with you. At the same time, cut some slack for your closed Amps, so they can get out there in the fast lane and do what they do best – fly!

The Sperm That Won

So, whether Amp or Vamp, is anybody capable of taking that extra step beyond ordinary?

The answer to this question is most certainly a sky scraper size YES! The potential talent that all of us have is quite simply unquantifiable. That fact that we are here right now as the human being that we are, is certification that we are all indeed incredibly unique. Everyone around you is far more special than you can possibly imagine. The fact that we are all who we are is in itself an astonishing success story. All of us already are Olympic Gold Medallists.

Let's start right at the very beginning when you applied for the position of you and out of millions and millions of other applicants, you got the job. Yes, congratulations, you are the sperm that won! You may not realise it now, but let me tell you, you ending up as you was no mean feat.

What an epic race. As many as five hundred million competitors took part, not even knowing whether or not it was just another practice run. Launched with little pre-warning from their starting blocks, literally swimming for their lives as they raced along at speeds averaging nine centimetres per hour. Mostly uphill, through chicanes and round hairpin bends and having to wag their tails more than sixteen thousand times in this gruelling challenge to be the first to reach that illusive egg. This was a dog eat dog, no holds barred, life and death struggle for survival. A winner takes all race – to be you!

And just think, whilst they were all paddling away like mad, at the same time around the world, there were zillions of others competing in countless other genealogical races, fighting just as hard as you did, only to end up as a goat or a badger.

Yes, the fact that you got the job as you and that you are here right now is nothing short of a miracle, each and every one of us really is, one in millions.

We all have unlimited and vastly unexplored potential, it's just that to realise our potential we all need to have the right guidance, the right environment and be given the opportunity to grow.

'To realise our potential we all need to have the right guidance, the right environment and be given the opportunity to grow.'

So who are these one-time one in a million winners that we are now trying to wake and inspire to take the next step with us?

Well the scary truth is that they probably don't even know themselves. They've most likely never had a chance or been given an opportunity to discover who they really are and what they're capable of. The reason for this is because all of us, not long after literally bursting on to the scene became conditioned by other people's beliefs. We were captured, rounded up, and sent to school!

Up until the point of entering through the school gates we all had, by the shed load, all the raw, natural ingredients that all the most successful people in the world have. We were full of life, literally fizzing with energy and free of all mental barriers. The chances back then of us ever being in danger of going anywhere near Planet Complacency and becoming Sleepwalkers was nil. In fact, our parents spent huge chunks of their lives desperately trying to get us off to sleep!

Then one day everything changed, and the conditioning began. We were entered into the narrow education system as a 150 mega watts child and came out as 40 watts adult.

After years of research for my first book and continued research since into the highest achieving Polar Bear Pirates around the world I've discovered that they all have in common eight basic ingredients:

- **They ask questions.** They're not tell people, they are outward looking ask people. They have a thirst for knowledge and a genuine, curious interest in everything around them. Have you ever spent an evening with someone who just talks about themselves, then at the end of the evening they turn round to you and say 'Well that's enough about me, what do you think of me?'

- **They are extremely enthusiastic about life and have a real passion for whatever they do.** I've noticed that successful people are always pointing out the things they love, whereas the less successful are always pointing out the things they don't like.

- **They have bottomless reserves of determination.** As true Polar Bear Pirates, they regard rejection and criticism as an accolade that they are not just sitting in the audience, but are taking part and actually doing something with their blip of time on this planet.

- **They have DIY belief – do it yourself belief.** They don't hang around waiting for others to achieve things to see that they are achievable.

- **They are doers.** Whilst others are wasting their time discussing and pondering things, they're out there already doing it and stealing the opportunity from under the noses of talkers.

- **They have incredible energy.** So much so that they have become human magnets attracting both success and luck.

- **They have a very simple, clear, untarnished 360 degree, 3D view of what they are trying to achieve.** They can spot opportunities that most people wouldn't spot if you sprayed them on their eyeballs.

- **As firm believers in life before death, they know how to have fun!**

Two decades to discover such basic things! Now having done all this research, something starts to really irritate me. Subconsciously I begin to realise that there is someone in my life who has all of these in abundance but I just can't put my finger on who that person is.

I start thinking about all the people that I've ever worked with or socialised with but I still can't think of who it is. Then one evening I'm at home watching TV when suddenly my six year old son Seb comes rocketing into the lounge.

Bouncing up and down and hopping from one foot to the other he suddenly exclaimed 'Is it true, is it really true Dad?!' I said 'Is what true?' He said 'Are we really really really going to the beach tomorrow?' I said 'Yes we're really really really going to the beach tomorrow!'

As he shot out of the room to tell the whole world it hit me like a brick between the eyes, I'd been looking in the wrong direction. The ingredients of all the most successful people in the world are the ingredients of a young child!!

Have you ever lawfully spent any time around young children? If you have you'll most certainly recognise in them all the natural ingredients they'll ever need to be a huge success.

- Do they ever stop asking questions? I read once that a typical four year old asks on average four hundred and thirty seven questions a day. I didn't know it was so few!

- How much enthusiasm do they have? 'Are we half way there yet?' 'First to see the sea!'

- Determination. Have you ever known of a young child ask for something and not end up getting it?

- Belief. They believe in tooth fairies and Father Christmas. They believe in life!

- They are doers, they just get on with things. They don't wake up slowly like us adults. As soon as their eyes pop open their very first thought is 'Oh good I'm here again, let's go!'

- The energy!! If you could hook up kids to the national grid, the world's energy supply problems would instantly be solved.

- They have such a simple, refreshing, and uninhibited outlook on life. They can't see any obstacles in their way.

- Fun?! I don't know about the children you may have in your life but if they're anything like my two youngest, Harry and Rosie, they just can't get enough of it!

Think about it, when's the last time you ever heard a young child turn around to you and say 'It's gonna rain later!' It will never happen!

Yes, we were all once brimming over with all these natural ingredients; we were all budding, mini Polar Bear Pirates!

And then, the conditioning started, we got thrown into life's big blender to come out the same as everyone else. We became prisoners of other people's thinking.

To check how much you have been conditioned over the years just do me a quick favour and fold your arms. Now, as quick as you can, fold them the other way. It feels odd doesn't it? That's because you've always done it a certain way and you've become conditioned to do it that way. Change always feels a bit strange at first.

If as a leader I'm going to motivate a group of people to pull together and deliver extraordinary results as one big team, I will need to smash open and dispel any restrictive conditioning that over the years may have wrapped itself around them and which, if not removed, will prevent them from shining like they once used to. I will need to dismantle all the imaginary barriers that were in the main created for good reason at the time to keep us 'little devils' in line!

To do that, I will need everyone, including myself to start doing some around walls, corkscrew thinking, looking at the world with childlike vision, seeing things differently and exploring new ways of doing them.

If we really are to differentiate ourselves from our competition I will need to give everyone the chance to release all the natural qualities that they once had as young children.

I most certainly don't want my people being the same as everyone else. I want everyone in my team to have the opportunity to discover their own unique character and their real talents. Above all else, I want them to have the chance to discover for the first time since applying for the position of them and getting it, just who they really are and what they are capable of. It's time to release the prisoners!

Some great news – All Sleepwalkers still have deep down inside them all the qualities they need to move on and reach Fat City. They may have been contained but they haven't gone away, we just need to release them.

TNT Sticky Picture Bombs — Handle With care!

W hen it comes to motivating people and creating fantastic customer service experiences, there are no more powerful weapons in your armoury than TNTs. The effect they can have on people is phenomenal.

TNTs for me, having spent most of my career trying to get the very best out of teams on shoe string budgets and steal business from much bigger competitors, are everything. They are what inspire people, the engagers, the secret weapons of great leaders and of any team that in pursuit of excellence, has become addicted to delivering exceptional customer service.

They are Tiny Noticeable Things. They may be tiny but they are highly explosive, they make an instant, massive, impact. They create the biggest, longest lasting pictures and the wonderful thing is, they cost nothing!

TNTs are what people see and what people remember. We will all be remembered long after we've gone for just a couple of TNTs. Regarded by most people as too petty to mention especially at exit interviews, these are the things that connect, motivate or de-motivate people. These are the tiny things that we all notice about each other that either please us or wind us right up!

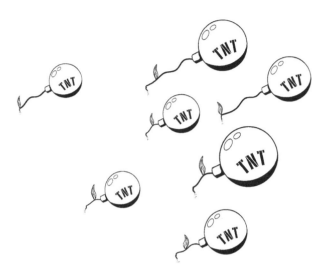

TNTs make and break relationships. Ask a marriage guidance counsellor why marriages break up after so many long years. Is it because of big things? No! It's all the little things like leaving the loo seat up, 'using my razor to shave her legs', wet towels left on beds, leaving dirty dishes on the side instead of putting them in the dishwasher, swigging milk straight from the carton and then putting it back in the fridge.

One little thing that drives me nuts is when I meet someone who can't stop continuously drawing imaginary speech marks in the air with their fingers to emphasise a particular word, for example 'We had such a "cool" time last night'. I've noticed recently that some people seem to have been on the advanced course and as well as using imaginary inverted commas, they have a habit of drawing a question mark in the air with their index finger whenever they ask you a question. Now that just sends me nuclear thermo.

To understand why TNTs have such an instant, powerful and emotional effect on people, we need to have a quick look at how the mind works from a Polar Bear Pirate perspective.

Firstly our minds don't speak English, Chinese, Japanese, French, Dutch, German, Hindi, Spanish, Thai, Korean, Russian, Italian or any other language for that matter, they work in pictures. Motivation, no matter what language people speak, is all about painting pictures in people's minds.

Protecting our mind is a grid. This grid is designed to stop us taking in big things and to help protect our hard drive from information overload. Without this front of house filter we would end up having massive heart attacks every time we experienced something big and terrible.

Believe you me, as an ex police officer, when you have to go to someone's house, someone who you've never met before, and deliver the very worst imaginable news, you hardly get your patrol car out of second gear. The reason being is you're trying to drive as slowly as you possibly can, knowing full well that at the end of your short journey you're going to meet a family you've never met before and deliver two sentences of news that are going to destroy this family's life forever. You keep looking down at your radio, hoping a miracle is going to happen and that you won't have to do this.

You pull up outside with the neighbours all peering out of their windows. You check, you double check and you treble check that you have the right address. You smarten yourself up and walk up to the front door, hoping in your heart of hearts that they're not in. You ring the door bell and knock. The door eventually opens and at that precise moment in time, being a police officer becomes the very worst job in the world.

You check that you have the right person and ask if you can come in. You follow them in, checking that no children are within earshot. Looking this person that you've never met before in the eyes, you deliver as best you can, your two sentences of news.

The initial reaction you can expect in most cases is just stunned silence. And this awful silence just seems to go on forever. The reason is the news you've just delivered cannot begin to be taken in. It is far too big.

So why do I make this point so aggressively to you? Because as a person who has spent years trying to inspire teams on tight budgets and as a person who has spent years pinching opportunities from under the noses of the competition, I cannot stress enough to you the explosive, emotional effects of TNTs.

The bigger organisations become and the more profitable they are, the more they seem to concentrate on big things to motivate staff and big things to win and keep customers. These big things don't have the impact that they think they do, they are too big to be taken in.

TNTs on the other hand are so small that they are able to go straight through the protective grid and directly impact onto the hard drive of people's minds.

I'll give you an example of just how explosive TNTs can be. I was at a conference in Antwerp in May 2004. The company organising it had themed it around Polar Bear Pirates and the afternoon was dedicated to TNTs. They were focusing on how they as a company could put customers at the heart of everything they do. They wanted to really take a look at themselves through the eyes of customers and as a result, improve relationships with them.

They invited members of the audience to come up on stage and share a TNT experience. A volunteer came up on stage and told us all a story that he said was a true story and which just stuck in my head. He said that a businessman with the help and support of his wife had tried for years to get a business off the ground. After many years of trying and having remortgaged their house, they'd eventually begun to reap the success that they deserved.

Having never had a brand new car and now for the first time in his life having money in the bank, he decided to go and choose one. It ended up being a tossup between a Mercedes and a Lexus. In the end after much discussion he decided to go for the Mercedes.

Seventy thousand pounds worth of Mercedes was delivered to his driveway and he was soon driving around in it as excited as a kid at Christmas. Suddenly to his horror, he noticed it was missing the cigarette lighter, something that probably costs less than a litre of fuel in a seventy thousand pound car. His friends said they'd never seen him get so upset before over such a small thing, especially they said, when you take into account that he doesn't even smoke!

He immediately phoned up Mercedes and they promised that they'd get it sorted for him.

By chance, the very same day, the Lexus salesperson phoned him in the office to see if he'd reached a decision yet on his choice of cars. Feeling slightly embarrassed he explained to them that he had just taken delivery of a Mercedes. Instantly the Lexus salesperson responded by saying that any Mercedes is a tremendous car to own and asked him if he was pleased with it. He said he was happy but also told them the story of the missing cigarette lighter. Without hesitation the Lexus salesperson pointed out that Mercedes were normally extremely good when it came to customer service and assured him that he was sure that they would soon sort it out for him.

The Lexus salesperson at the end of the conversation asked him if he would reconsider buying a Lexus when it came round to picking another new car in the future, he said he certainly would.

Having left his office that evening he arrived home to find that his wife and family were still out. Just as he put his key in the front door he was surprised to see his neighbour come bounding up his drive, out of breath and with a big parcel in her hands. This lovely lady from next door explained that a delivery driver had called around to his house about an hour earlier with the parcel but because nobody was in, she had signed for it and taken it home with her.

He thanked her and took the parcel through into his kitchen where he opened it. There in the middle of the parcel was a shoebox, in the shoebox was a mountain of cotton wool, and nestling on the top of the cotton wool was the Mercedes cigarette lighter. Underneath the cotton wool was a compliment slip that simply said 'With very best wishes – your Lexus salesman.'

BANG!! These are the things that blow competition out of the water!

I'd like to stress at this point that I'm not sponsored by Lexus! But, having said this, I was delivering a workshop shortly after hearing this story and I used it as TNT example. The MD of the company who was holding this workshop session told me that he had just traded in his old Jaguar for a new Lexus and that what blew him away more than anything else was that when he got in his new Lexus, he discovered to his absolute delight that they had tuned in all his favourite radio stations that he'd had tuned in, in his old Jag!

TNTs are the things that create dazzling, world class customer service but they are also the little things that differentiate a world class leader from a fire fighting manager. **Why? Because they either show people that you care or that you don't.**

In January 2006 I was on an aeroplane flying out to a conference in Tenerife, I was sitting next to a South African businessman who shared with me a gem of a TNT story.

He told me that recently whilst on a flight from South Africa to the USA he had had an amazing TNT experience. He explained that during the flight he was deeply engrossed in reading a really good book when he gradually became aware of excited voices and some sort of commotion going on a few rows behind him. He couldn't see what it was so he continued to read his book. The noise and commotion got nearer and nearer and suddenly he was aware of a passenger standing over him. He looked up to find himself looking at Nelson Mandela. Nelson Mandela smiled at him, held out his hand and said 'Good afternoon, my name is Nelson Mandela, I just wanted to come and say hello to you'.

It transpired later that despite being in his late eighties, Nelson Mandela had gone round and met every single passenger on that aeroplane and said hello.

Nelson Mandela is without doubt one of the greatest leaders of our time, probably the greatest. His ability to reach out, to connect with and 'touch' people at all levels is what sets him apart.

WARNING: TNTs like any explosive products need to be handled with great care. Yes, they can 'touch' people, create wonderful impressions and leave behind positive pictures that can last a lifetime. But, as well as creating positive experiences, they can also easily create very different experiences.

A well intended positive TNT can, if not thought through properly, end up as Tiny Negative Thing. This occurs when a TNT instead of having the desired effect of creating a fond memory backfires and explodes in the face of the person delivering it. The result is that instead of having a fond memory the recipient ends up not being 'touched' but slapped in the face by it and left with an unforgettable, painful memory.

I was doing some leadership work for a very large, well known company. Over dinner a lady who requested that her and her company's name both remain anonymous told me about a Tiny Negative Thing that she had once experienced. She explained that for four years solid she had worked very closely with her manager. Their roles meant that they travelled together an awful lot and stayed away in hotels at least a couple of nights a week. She was quick to assure me that it was purely a working relationship but it did mean that they had probably seen more of each other during that time than they had their partners.

One day her manager came into her office and announced that he was moving on to pastures new and that he had come to thank her for four great years. He told her how much he'd enjoyed working with her and that he couldn't have worked with a more wonderfully supportive person. He then went on to express just how much, in a professional way, she meant to him.

He then pulled out from behind his back a surprise thank you gift, a bottle of vintage champagne. As he handed it to her he kissed on the cheek and gave her a bit of an awkward hug. He thanked her again and quickly left.

She told me that unable to contain her emotions, her eyes began watering up as she stood there in the middle of her office holding this fine bottle of champagne.

She said 'Adrian, I'm teetotal'.

He'd stood in front of her telling her how much he cared about her and yet in four years he'd never even noticed that she's never touched a drop of alcohol. Just one TNT had painted a very big picture.

As a complete contrast to this, I was speaking to a delegate in the coffee break at a recent conference in Wales and she told me, with great delight and uncontainable excitement that her manager Wendy was the very best boss in the whole wide world! Adding that she wouldn't want to work for anyone else. When I asked why, she explained that she and her husband only have a garden the size of a handkerchief but they are both mad keen gardeners. As a thank you for all her hard work over the past few weeks, her boss Wendy had only gone and got them both tickets for the Chelsea Flower Show.

TNTs have to be relevant and they have to be kept up. For example, people at leadership and team building workshops often come up with the idea of sending everyone in their team a birth-day card. A lovely idea, but this has to be kept up, someone has to make sure everybody gets a card and someone has to make sure it gets posted on the right day. The day that someone doesn't get a card is the day that you have someone on their birthday feeling a bit left out and slightly deflated. What was intended as a positive experience has ended up, for one person anyway, a negative one.

A negative TNT that I've heard a couple of managers come out with is when an enthusiastic new starter goes up to them all excited about a new idea that they've had and their manager turns around and says 'We tried that, it didn't work'. The new starter walks away looking and feeling about three inches shorter.

Never commit to anything whilst on the hop. Now and again your people may try and catch you in between things or when you're in wind down mode. For example when you're going out the door on your way home, knowing it's a good time to ask you a big favour. On the spur of the moment and in a more relaxed mood, there is more chance of you saying 'Yes, go for it!'

Then later on it may suddenly occur to you that for whatever reason, you shouldn't have agreed to it. You now have to go back to them, make a U turn and let them down. My standard response to anyone putting me in this situation used to be 'Let me take it away with me so I can give it some thought and get back to you tomorrow morning'. This way I buy myself time to think it through and hopefully I can give them the good news the next day. Even if I go back to them with a no, I haven't as their manager disappointed them as much as I would have done by going back on a promise.

Both positive and negative TNTs create very different emotions. They can instantly make people feel special, wanted, thanked, included, recognised, validated, respected and they can very easily make people feel unwanted, disappointed, let down, left out, angry, disrespected or second class.

I've met some highly intelligent senior managers over the years who, despite being passionate about their business and working extremely hard, have never been able to really connect with their people because they've either completely under estimated the power of TNTs or because they are such small basic things they've overlooked them.

TNTs are what people see. You as a leader can work your bottles off behind a wall or a closed door but your people won't see it. If you do want to show people you care and you do want to engage them, some of the simplest things that people tell me they notice and really appreciate are their managers:

- asking how they are now and again and then actually listening to the answer;

- saying 'Thank you';

- smiling and saying things like 'Good morning';

- answering the phone, rolling up their sleeves and getting stuck in when short staffed;

- doing some of the less popular little jobs around the place, like washing up coffee cups;

All such simple things but sadly a lot of managers just don't seem to get them.

If you're going to thank someone, don't do it as you just happen to walk past them on the way out of the door, this dilutes and cheapens your thanks because they will see it as an impulse thank you. Be seen to go out of your way to thank people and then go back to where you were. It will have a more powerful, lasting effect.

The higher up TNTs come from the more explosive they seem to be when they land. In other words the more senior the manager is that drops the TNT, the more of an impact it is likely to have. So if say a Chief Executive stops and has a quick chat with a junior member of staff, uses their first name, asks about their family, how things are going and then listens to them, it is quite likely to have a powerful effect.

TNTs are also particularly powerful when they come from people who are not perceived by customers as being in customer facing roles but who are regarded as being backroom staff. For example, when a cleaner vacuuming a floor in a hotel, suddenly looks up, smiles and says 'Good morning, how are you?' A great little, surprise TNT. That is of course, if it is in the morning!

Amongst many, some of the TNT ideas teams have come up with in my workshops to help make their working environment a little bit more interesting, bond teams together, get people more involved and show some recognition are things like:

- Cakes On Wednesdays, managers bring their staff cakes into the office.

- Managers giving up their car parking spaces to those who don't have one but who have really stepped beyond ordinary.

- Five A Day Days, everyone brings in some fruit to share.

- 59.59 meetings, make it a rule that no meeting should ever last more than 59 minutes and 59 seconds!

- A day or perhaps half a day off for someone when it's their birthday.

- Hand written thank you notes that really stand out from the millions of emails that we all receive each day.

- Butty Starts, managers provide an assortment of butties first thing in the morning for when their people arrive for work.

- A team montage picture on the wall.

- Job Swaps, team members (including managers) swap roles for a day.

- A team photo made into a jigsaw puzzle and everyone is given a piece to show that without them it's not a complete picture.

- Family Visits Days, staff can bring their partners and kids in so they can see where they work and meet a few of their team mates.

All very simple but they do put a few smiles on a few faces.

At one workshop the MD of a company shared with everyone, a lovely little staff retention TNT. When he joined his company at the age of sixteen, like most people when they first join any company, he was apprehensive, slightly nervous and wandering if he was fitting in okay. Then one day, having been there only a few weeks he received a handwritten note delivered to him at his home address. The note simply said 'Just a quick note to say that I'm already hearing some tremendous things about you, I'm really looking forward to working with you over the coming years'. It was signed by his then Managing Director.

He told us all that whenever over the past thirty-two years he's been head hunted, he's found himself pulling that note out from the bottom of the drawer in his study at home, reading it and thinking 'No thanks, you can keep your job, I belong here'.

He explained that now he is the MD he posts a similar hand written note to all the new starters in his company. He said that retention rates had gone through the roof.

Talking of hand written notes, some friends of ours having just got back from spending a week in a fabulous hotel in Switzerland were bowled over when upon arriving home they discovered a hand written letter amongst all their post from hotel's General Manager thanking them for staying at his hotel and hoping that they'd had a good journey home. Bang!

As well as falling into two distinct groups, positive and negative, TNTs are also incredibly sticky things. In fact they could be described as 'double sticky' for the following two reasons.

As positive or negative TNTs, they stick together. Once you notice a particular type of TNT, i.e. a positive or a negative, it is highly likely that you will start spotting more and more of the same kind and they are double sticky because both types of TNTs leave pictures behind that stick in the mind for a very long time.

However sod's law has it that TNTs are not all equal. Unfortunately Negative TNTs are a lot easier to spot, they are considerably more explosive and when it comes to sticking around in people's minds they are far stickier than positive ones. I would say that the average sticky power ratio between the two is around about 25 to 1.

It takes at least three positive TNTs to create a good overall experience but just one negative TNT to create a bad one. It all depends which you notice first. If you spot a positive one first you are, as I said a moment ago likely to spot more positive ones and likewise if you spot a negative one first, you are far more likely to spot more negative ones. So always make sure you get a good one in first!

What increases the power ratio to 25 to 1 is that if you were to spot a few positive ones first and then spot just one negative one, that single negative one would cancel out all the positive ones. But if you saw a few negative ones first, it would take a whole army of positive TNTs to cancel them out.

What is worth remembering, especially if you are trying to build your business on the reputation of your customer service is that your customers are probably more likely to tell others about a negative TNT experience than they are a positive one!

Your people will be motivated or de motivated by what they see and the biggest pictures are created by the smallest of things, TNTs. Never ever as a leader underestimate for one moment the profound, lasting effects that these little things can have on people.

'Your people will be motivated or de motivated by what they see and the biggest pictures are created by the smallest of things, TNTs.'

TNTs are indeed what make the difference. They are a visible difference between four and five star service, managers and leaders, ordinary and extraordinary. They help create a little bit of magic and as I keep on reminding everyone – they cost nothing!

Why Wake Up For You?

'm sorry to disappoint and I know I'm sounding like a bit of a Neg Ferret here when I tell you there is no easy answer to this. I'm not exaggerating when I tell you that if you want to wake your people, inspire them to burst free from their conditioning and step beyond ordinary with you, you're going to have to differentiate yourself from other managers; you are going to have to become not just a leader but a Polar Bear Pirate leader!

Being a good leader means that as well as fully using all your natural childlike qualities and mastering TNTs, you are going to have to have all the additional qualities that all good leaders have.

Waking some people and getting them to realise that they have been sleepwalking can at times seem almost impossible. Facing up to the fact that they are not really giving it their best is something that not everyone is going to find easy to admit to themselves, let alone their boss.

Waking them will mean having to gain their trust and this will only be achieved through honesty and you putting some trust in them. And, if you want them not only to trust you but to follow you, you're going to have to display the optimism of Martin Luther King, the innovative skills of the Romans, the caring talents of Mother Teresa, the passion of a secret lover, the sales skills of a good parent, the persistence of a cat herder and the patience of a goldfish trainer.

On top of these entry level requirements into the world of leadership you will have to ensure you provide your people with the tools to enable them to take the extra step. And, at the same time you're going to have to display the energy levels of kids on sugar, constantly shining far brighter than anyone else around you, especially on that wet Monday morning when you've had the weekend from hell and you're feeling like you've slept in a wheelie bin.

You'll have to be prepared to make some spectacular mistakes and, I hate to point this out, but you'll be surprised how many managers seem to forget this, it's a good idea if you want people to follow you, to be seen to take that first step, first.

If you then want to step beyond being a good leader and into the realms of being an extraordinary leader, you are going to have to show your people just what they are capable of by helping them learn to trust not only you, but themselves.

Not as easy as it may sound when you take into account that to start with, many of them won't have anything like the belief that they'll need to take the first few steps with you because they've probably never ever been given the opportunity to take them before.

Then, just when you do think everyone is on board and following you, you're going to have to be prepared to be let down by the very people you thought would be the last people in the world to let you down.

And remember, even if you are prepared and equipped for all this, they will only wake up and follow you, if they choose to.

Welcome to leadership! I told you it's not going to be easy, but it's worth it. For me there is no better feeling than watching someone who not so long ago had very little belief in themselves suddenly start to grow as an individual and begin to make a real difference as a key member of the team.

'There is no better feeling than watching someone who not so long ago had very little belief in themselves suddenly start to grow as an individual and begin to make a real difference as a key member of the team.'

So why will it be so difficult to wake them? Well the answer lies in just two words: 'Comfortable' and 'Safe'. These are the two main weapons of Planet Complacency.

To entice visitors, induce them into sleep mode and then keep them as its unsuspecting guests, Planet Complacency has put a spin on the conditioning experienced by everyone during their school years. This fiendishly clever con trick has made it hard for its victims to face up to seeing their own conditioning for what it really is.

Instead of seeing it as being held back by other people's beliefs, they regard the imaginary obstacles that surround them, not as restrictive barriers but as some sort of protective blanket.

In other words by playing on their fear of failure, it has spun what is in effect a prison into a safe haven for them to hide in. Victims even tell themselves that they'd like to move on but the truth is, deep down, they don't really believe they can. Like members of some weird cult they're quite happy staying put, cocooned within their comfy confines.

To get them to open their eyes and realise that they are in the process of being suckered in and robbed of all their potential, we as leaders need to start encouraging them to bin their imaginary comfort blankets, to see things for what they really are, have some belief in themselves and to start doing things that they'd never thought possible.

One of the reasons people have become 'guests' of Planet Complacency is because they have fallen into cosy routines. They have just got too used to things, become too familiar with it all, have stood still, got their slippers on and lost focus. To get them out of sleep mode and refocused we need to get them kicking off their slippers and moving forward again by giving them fresh, stimulating, widget detonating challenges to agitate their minds and give them a bit of a bump start.

These new challenges, if they are to re energise them and stretch their abilities, will involve them having to draw upon all their talents and it will of course require them to try doing things differently, things that to begin with, are going to feel uncomfortable.

It will also mean, if we are to stir the status quo, people sharing and being prepared at times to put their own personal ambitions to one side for the greater good of the team, and it will often mean going against popular Herd Head opinion, which for most people will certainly feel a bit odd.

They may even have to take a step back and in some cases, revisit Rock Bottom. And it will inevitably expose them to the likelihood of experiencing their worst nightmare – failure.

However, in every case it is achievable and the further away you manage to move them away from it, the weaker Planet Complacency's seductive powers become.

It's staying away from Planet Complacency that any successful person will tell you is the hard bit. To keep your people away and avoid its lethal draw, you and your people can't afford to stand still for one moment.

You yourself are going to have to be highly innovative to keep your team engaged, wide awake, focused and on the front foot. As an innovator you'll have to be constantly prepared to change, and at times, change quickly.

Everything in this universe is continually changing, nothing is ever standing still, now has already gone. Think of anyone who has been successful and who has managed to stay at the top of their game, they will have changed. Those who are able to anticipate, adapt quickest to and see opportunity within change, will always be the winners.

Today, when I look at some of the people that I once looked up to and admired as great innovators, I'm often disappointed. The reason being, they haven't moved on. Their style, approach and whole way of thinking just doesn't seem to have changed and what used to be seen as innovative, even radical, now appears like a once really flash car, like something out of The Stone Age.

They must have fallen hook, line and sinker for Planet Complacency's mesmeric beauty and taken up permanent residency there. Having once tasted considerable success and enjoyed the power trip that came with it, they probably began to regard themselves as so cool that they simply didn't need to move on.

Wallowing in their own success and not being able to see what was coming around the corner because of their XXXL size egos getting in the way, along with not having anyone around them wanting to lose their job by pointing out that they were losing touch, they must have become frozen in their own self perceived image. This being the case, as time went by and everything else around them changed, they would have become isolated and inevitably become fossilised, like some giant compliment eating dinosaur.

As a litmus test to check whether or not you yourself are losing touch, you should think about all the people around you and how you see yourself in relation to them. The day that you think for just one crotchet of a moment that you're a better person than the person who empties your bin at the end of the day, is the day you should re evaluate yourself and seriously consider doing something else.

I think one of the keys to successful leadership and to getting teams to deliver is not to just pay lip service to it but genuinely really grasp the fact that everyone in your team has something to offer. It is up to us as leaders to help them discover these talents and put them to good use.

The art of being a great leader, apart from giving clear direction is to give everyone a sense of belonging, to make everyone around you feel validated and good about themselves.

The best leader I have ever worked for was when I was a young police officer in St Pauls, Bristol. I was in his team, Group 2 Alpha Tango, during and after the riots there. Inspector Richard Allen, affectionately known as 'Twiggy' Allen was to say the least an inspirational leader.

I've never known a group of such diverse people show so much loyalty to one person nor want to give or do so much for someone. Besides having mega respect from all his team he was also in the extremely rare position of having the respect of the local community.

He was more passionate than anyone else about what we as a team were trying to achieve. He always seemed to have time for people and had a wonderful way of making all of us feel a bit special and part of something unique. He trusted us and supported us in our individual roles, and he never let us down. He allowed us under difficult circumstances to be ourselves. He let us take ownership and gave us responsibility but at the same time held us accountable for our actions. I remember him saying once that he believed in giving everyone a long lead but keeping it on a very tight grip!

Due to a lack of much needed resources he had become an expert in using innovative TNTs to engage us. He positively encouraged team members' individual personalities to shine through and he was an advocate of people having some fun, especially in tough times, probably to help us to cope with the darker sides of the job.

He had a real knack for always keeping us on our toes. You could never quite guess where he was coming from, there was never an opportunity for anyone to slow down and start sleepwalking!

A charismatic personality with incredible energy, always leading from the front, but what made him so extraordinary and probably why he was given so much respect from so many different quarters was that he genuinely cared about people.

If you show your people that you passionately care not only about them but also about what you are trying to achieve together, you'll be well on the way to opening their eyes and engaging them.

The bottom line is that provided that your people have a pulse, are in the right roles, are able to use whatever gifts they have, are having some fun, feeling good and knowing that you really do care, they will at some stage wake up and follow you.

My father used to say, 'Always judge someone by how they treat those around them from whom they have nothing to gain'.

Don't Do Perfect

would say from my experience that the main cause of most people's disengagement is their manager's inability to show people that they care, even if they do.

Whilst striving to be ultra efficient many managers become disconnected from their people and as a result end up being far less effective. Rather than spending time with their people and as a consequence driving the business forward, they just don't seem to realise how they appear through the eyes of their team, which is sadly all too often, too distant and too busy doing all the irrelevant things astonishingly well.

The best description that I've heard of the difference between being efficient and being effective is – "Being efficient is doing things right and being effective is doing the right things".

If managers are to become leaders and wake those who need waking, they will need to wake up themselves and in return for being more effective, stop trying to be quite so efficient. **People aren't ever going to be engaged by email, they need warmth, they need a human touch, they need you to be with them. Email is the biggest ally of Planet Complacency!**

Over efficient managers are like those poor souls sat in the cocktail bar of the Titanic, sipping their drinks, tapping their feet to the rhythm of the band and deliberating over whether or not they should have a nightcap, completely oblivious to the circumstances around them.

Some seem blind to the fact that their people are disengaged, only realising when it's too late and a resignation letter lands on their desk from one of their corner piece Amps.

If you are prepared to take that extra step yourself and show your people that you respect and genuinely care about them by spending time with them and listening to them, it's a mutual thing, they will in return start to respect you, care about you and want to spend time listening to you. If you don't, they won't, simple as that.

If you want to get the buy in of not only the Amps, Vamps, Sleepwalkers and possibly a few of the borderline Pothole People, you're going to have to be sure to always be one thing, and that's yourself.

If this along with TNTs is the only thing that you take away from this book, you won't have wasted your money buying it or your efforts borrowing or the kindness of someone who has given it to you.

If you try and be something that you aren't, people will see through you, they won't believe in you and they certainly won't give you their thumbs up.

I know this is such an obvious thing to remind you of but becoming someone we're not is like breathing. When people are doing it they just don't realise that they are doing it and now and again they need a little reminder, just like I've just reminded you that you are breathing, hopefully!

Seriously, so many managers end up falling flat on their faces and end up driving people not only towards Planet Complacency but towards the door by trying to be something or someone they are not.

At every leadership workshop I deliver I invite everyone in the room to give me a wish list of what they really need from their dream leader. After much thought provoking discussion, these twenty-six words amongst many others are the most popular words (in no particular order) to appear on the flip charts:

Trust
Honesty
Transparency
Communication
Direction
Passion
Reward
Listening
Understanding
Ownership
Responsibility
Feedback
Consistency
Fun

Inspiration
Belief
Challenged
Belong
Clarity
Fair
Validated
Encouragement
Support
Recognition
Loyalty
Respect

As you can see, people expect an awful lot from you! After much more discussion it is generally agreed that the one thing they really want and that jumps straight to the top of everyone's flip chart is time. More than anything else what people want from you as their leader is your time.

'More than anything else what people want from you as their leader is your time.'

I then ask the group what three words would best describe the perfect leader who is going to give them all of the above, including time. Eventually everything gets percolated down to just these three words: Strong, Caring and Fallible.

Strong is perhaps the more obvious one in that we all imagine a great leader as being strong, making decisions, supporting us, leading from the front, giving direction and challenging us. Unfortunately strong leadership is often wrongly associated with people being big and loud. This may be in some cases true and can work very well, if they are being themselves. But it is worth remembering that a lot of highly successful leaders are fairly quiet, low profile people who are just as strong, if not often stronger.

Caring, well I've already banged on about the virtues of showing you really care if you want to engage and motivate your people. It's the third one 'fallible' that for me, when I first started running these workshops was, until I really started thinking about it, the big surprise eye opener.

Think about the very best person you have ever worked for, why were they so good at motivating you?

People really would prefer to work for someone who is capable of making an error. They are more likely to connect with, relate to and be engaged by someone who has a hint of soul, who has flaws, defects, faults and makes mistakes. In other words someone just like them, someone who is human!

The key for any fallible person wanting people to follow them is to be quite open about their faults. Provided they are passionate about what they are trying to achieve and their faults don't affect their ability to perform well in their role, as far as their people are concerned, these human flaws really don't matter.

The real reason that we humans like people who are upfront about their faults is because we trust them and at the same time we are mistrusting of anyone and anything that appears to be perfect, quite simply because we find it hard to believe that perfect really exists.

Please don't get me wrong here, always relentlessly striving for perfection is an absolute entry level, no discussion must, for any self-respecting Polar Bear Pirate wanting to reach Fat City and be the very best at whatever it is they do, but someone trying to make out to their people that they themselves are perfect, well that's just something else!

There can be fewer things more disengaging or amusing than a manager pretending to be perfect. Instead of leading it they become the team's entertainment officer. Unable to ever laugh at themselves they end up providing at their own expense everyone around them with a few very good, behind their backs laughs.

Just like The Bermuda Triangle and The Loch Ness Monster, I would truly love to think that the perfect person does exist, but deep down inside, having personally not met one yet, I'm not sure they do.

The great news for us imperfect people is that there is hope for all of us becoming great leaders, so long as we stay strong, really care and don't pretend to be something we are not!

Always talk candidly with your team about your imperfections and be seen to be able to laugh at the more obvious ones.

SonAR Leaders

You'd be quite shocked at the number of times in coffee breaks at conferences or at workshops that I've had people whispering to me that they are thinking of looking for another job and the simple reason is, their manager no longer seems to care anymore. When I ask how they know that they don't care, invariably their answer is, 'Because they never seem to listen'.

The absurd thing is, when I suggest to them that they point this out to their manager and make their feelings known, their response is often what sounds like a punch line 'Oh I've tried that, but they didn't listen!'

Poor managers spend their time talking and looking for opportunities to catch people out. The world's most effective leaders, what I call SONAR leaders, spend their time listening and looking for opportunities to praise and thank people.

When I'm running workshops, I often ask those attending to draw their picture of Fat City, in other words, what does true success look like to them. Everybody draws a different picture.

Yet, when I'm at parties, I seem to have a habit of getting cornered in kitchens, trapped by the one person everyone else has managed to avoid or escape from. Having somehow found out what I do for a living and having had a few too many, they start trying to draw me into a 'heavy' conversation about motivation. This conversation invariably becomes more and more one way as they expound and spout out their theories on the subject.

Then as a build up to their killer line, they jab their finger in my chest and come up with, what for me, has to be one of the most painful lines ever uttered – 'I'll tell you the one thing that motivates everyone!'

I wait with toes firmly curled in my shoes, my hand now covering my drink, ninety-nine point nine percent sure that the very next word to come out of their mouth along with fragments of food is going to be one of the following five:

(1) 'Money!'

(2) 'Fear!'

(3) 'Power!'

(4) 'Love!'

(5) 'Sex!'

The reason that this person's statement gives me the same sensation as what I can only imagine chewing baking foil giving is because whichever of the five words this poor deluded Bloater chooses to use, they are going to be wrong. In fact if they were to use all five of these words, they would still be completely wrong.

The reason being is that all of us are different and we're all motivated by different things. To put things into context, it would be a thousand times easier trying to guess next week's winning lottery numbers than it would be trying to guess what motivates an individual.

Your ability to engage, inspire and show you really care will very much depend on your ability to listen.

SONAR stands for Sounding Out Needs And Responding.

SONAR Leadership is all about putting your head into other people's worlds, gaining a better understanding of where they're coming from and what makes them tick. **It's about looking for the best in people and bringing it out**.

One of the reasons why modern day submarines are so deadly is because of their ability to listen, take on board (excuse the pun) information and act on it.

It's exactly the same for Polar Bear Pirate leaders except that they're not focusing quite so much on listening out for enemy targets. Instead, they are finely tuned into, listening out for and honing in on opportunities to develop their teams, new ways to keep them moving on and innovative ideas for taking their already exceptional customer service experience to a whole new level. Their antennae are always switched on and their SONAR fully functioning as they constantly listen out for:

- The needs of their people.

- The needs of their customers.

- Ideas.

- Opportunities.

- Which 'hot buttons' to push to motivate each individual person.

- How they can mould teams and inspire everyone to pull together.

- Potential skills and talents of those around them.

- Better ways to engage people.

- If people are in exactly the right roles.

- How they can better empower their people.

- Are their Amps well placed to look after their Vamps?

- Opportunities to deploy relevant TNTs.

- Ways to improve the working environment.

- If their people are happy and growing in the right direction.

- Exciting challenges to keep people progressing.

- Market openings.

- Changes needed to improve performance.

- The hum of 'Hummers'.

- What's coming around the corner?

- How they themselves are performing.

- What they could be doing differently.

But it's not just about listening, it's about responding to the information that you receive. It's about recognising good performance
but it's also about challenging poor performance. You must be
prepared to face up to and confront things that you come across
and that you're not happy with.

'It's not just about listening, it's about respond-ing to the information that you receive.'

You also have to be careful of how you react to potentially duff
information fed to you deliberately by those playing politics or
those with long standing prejudices and personal gripes against
others. It's important to filter out broad sweeping, popular but
non factual opinions and whatever you do, try and avoid being
drawn in by malicious gossip being promoted by The Pothole
People.

Polar Bear Pirates use two types of SONAR. Passive and proactive. Passive simply involves taking a step back, listening and
gathering information. Then once you have all the information at
your finger tips, acting on it.

I'd highly recommend this type of low key SONAR to any leader
in the early stages of taking over a new team or moving into a
new working environment or even a new culture that they are
unfamiliar with. The last thing they'll need to do in this situation
is go blundering in and end up muddying the waters of what is
likely to be an already unclear situation.

Proactive SONAR which can be a lot of fun and throw up some very interesting findings if you do it well is all about probing, questioning, challenging and bouncing ideas and thoughts around, then listening to see what comes back.

A few great SONAR Leaders:

- **Queen Elizabeth I**

  This brilliantly successful monarch took great care in listening out for talent and surrounding herself with extremely capable people. Strong, determined and intelligent but what set her apart and made her so popular was her ability to sound out and act on the advice on those she trusted. Elizabeth stayed honed in to the feelings of her people throughout her long reign, always keeping an open mind and being prepared to change a policy if it got the big thumbs down.

- **Sir Ernest Shackleton**

  Described as 'the greatest leader that ever came on God's earth bar none'. He made time to be with and listen to his crew and their concerns. He was able to connect with everyone around him and had a beyond genius ability to motivate each individual. Encouraging fun, he was able to create an environment where his men felt good in mind bogglingly harsh circumstances.

- **Dame Anita Roddick**

  A passionate personality who would spend as much time as possible in all areas of her organisation, visiting the factory floor, actively taking part in meetings, talking and listening to, caring for, growing and inspiring her people. Anita Roddick loved to challenge her teams, generate corkscrew thinking, stretch people's abilities and fire up their imaginations.

- **Sir Richard Branson**

  This phenomenally successful believer in life before death is forever gaining input from others and listening and tuning into what they have to say. Yes, he has a natural, almost magical gift for engaging with everyone he comes into contact with but he is also what I would describe as a master of SONAR leadership. He carries a notebook around with him at all times as he listens to friends, employees, business people and total strangers, knowing full well that the next great idea could come from anywhere at any moment.

It's a good idea particularly when solution finding to use your number one natural childlike ingredient and ask around with as many people as possible. It's often very surprising where some of the best solutions come bouncing back from.

Developing Their Pictures Together

Our minds work in pictures, what Polar Bear Pirates call Power Of Picture or POP. The attitude that someone has towards something is purely the picture in their mind that they have taken of it.

As I said earlier, motivation is all about painting pictures and the key to motivating people to achieve their goals is to help them develop their own pictures and not try and paint yours into their minds. If you have any dealings with teenagers you will know that trying to paint your pictures into their minds is an even bigger waste of time than asking them to tidy their room.

It's exactly the same with some of your staff. It's just that because you're their boss and probably not their Mum or Dad, unlike teenage kids they are being polite to you and at times only pretending to listen!

Polar Bear Pirates use SONAR to try and understand their people's aspirations and then inspire them to achieve them. They do this by encouraging their people to start popping pictures. They help their people develop and focus on personal pictures of small goals that they'd like to achieve not only in but also outside of work. Each time they 'pop' one of these pictures they take another step forwards towards their Fat City.

What's important is that individuals have their own pictures, in some cases actual photos or pictures down loaded off the internet, cut out of magazines or brochures. No matter how odd, weird, funny, random or boring you may think they are, so long as they are their pictures, that they have chosen, they'll be inspired. And, the more vivid they are the more chance there is of them being 'popped'.

I've had people in the past who have been underperforming but as a result of suddenly having their own pictures to focus on of real, tangible, out of work things that they particularly needed or really wanted, they all started performing extremely well in work, some even surprising themselves! The list of pictures has included (purely from memory here!): Hoovers, dishwashers, clothes, drum kits, cookers, pets, bicycles, plants, cars, surf boards, memberships to health clubs, garden furniture, evening classes, TVs, perfumes, taking their family away for a weekend break, cameras, dog training classes, irons, go karts, upholstery courses, lawn mowers, woks, having their teeth whitened, tennis rackets, tickets to concerts, riding lessons, a harp, aquariums, watches, a new bed, barbeques, Easter eggs, music lessons, train sets, cookery classes, children's car seats, acting classes, bouncy castles, coffee machines, tap dance lessons, microwaves, golf lessons, ski poles, wardrobes, scuba diving courses, sofas, jewellery, fridge freezers, holidays, season tickets, charity walks/cycle rides, a wedding dress and of course cuddly toys!

All very different pictures that belonged to very different people but the positive effect that they all had on their owners was quite amazing.

When goal setting, it is a lot more effective if people sit down with you and with your guidance, along with their pictures, set their own goals with you. Make sure they make a commitment to both themselves and to you. This way, having taken owner-ship of them and given a commitment, they are much more likely to achieve them. People tend to work a lot harder towards achieving these 'own goals', especially when they've set them with the input, help and support of others. That little widget of fear comes into play, imparting an added impulse that just gives them that extra urge to want to get popping.

Grow people gradually by making sure they only have teaspoon size tasters of success, i.e. small goals. Put the tablespoons away and encourage them to take little steps so they gradually grow in confidence and begin liking themselves. Please note: You want people to like themselves not love themselves, otherwise they'll have no friends!

'Grow people gradually by making sure they only have teaspoon size tasters of success, i.e. small goals.'

If you try and get them to take giant leaps they are likely to experience failure and end up feeling deflated and disappointed. Feed them little tasters of success, not big, hard to swallow mouthfuls which are only likely to leave behind a bitter taste.

A lot of people are able to describe their idea of true success, i.e. their picture of Fat City to me. Unfortunately so many people never get to see it. One of the main reasons for this is that apart from not being able to picture a path to it, those who do have a path don't have enough exciting little goals to picture and look forward to popping along the way.

Polar Bear Pirates refer to it as 'Bubble Wrapping' which they use to keep their people motivated and focused. Having found out what someone's picture of Fat City looks like, they help them lay down a clear path to it, a path littered along the way with lots of little personal picture goals. Then to prevent them from drifting off it towards Planet Complacency they keep them awake, buzzing and always moving on and looking forwards by continuously encouraging and helping them to develop new pictures to pop along the way. This way they are hopefully able to keep all their team on course and heading together towards their shared, big team picture of Fat City.

Polar Bear Pirates call the little picture goals along this 'Bubble Wrap Path' Smugs because when you walk along it and start popping your pictures it gives you the same lovely smug sensation that walking bare foot on and popping bubble wrap gives you.

Making Time and Space for the Big Doable Stuff

have come to the conclusion that in many cases a lot of managers just don't know how to lead. They don't know where to begin when it comes to engaging those around them and having almost given up, they themselves have succumbed to the comfort and safety of Planet Complacency.

As a result they tend to end up not even managing but merely coping. Some turn into serial meeting goers and combat typists, flapping around like moths at fairgrounds, firing out emails, playing politics and lurching from one quarter to the next, generating whole forest loads of mind boggling reports in a smoke screen attempt to hide their ineffectiveness and justify their existence.

In fact it would seem some will do just about anything, so long as it doesn't involve spending time with their people. The funny thing is, whenever anyone confronts them about finding some time to be with their people, they all come up with the same excuse that they've got too much on their plate.

Have you ever noticed how top sports people seem to have all the time and space in the world? If you were to watch a local Sunday league football match it would most likely appear to be quite a frantic affair with lots of people all running around, hoofing a ball up and down and shouting at each other. In contrast if you were to see some of the best players in the world playing, despite the pace of the game being so much faster, they all seem to have time and space around them to be able to think and most of the time, display enviable control. It's the same in tennis. The top players appear to glide around the court hardly breaking into a sweat, whereas in comparison, those at my local tennis club always appear to be scurrying around like pigs on skates, huffing and puffing and making it all look like such hard work.

The same goes for the best leaders in the world, they all seem to have time and space to focus in on the important things. The truth is that all these top people whether they're in business or in sport deliberately make time and space, that's why they're so good!

I'm not generally a huge fan of politicians and whenever they're not answering a simple question with a straight answer, which these days seems to be pretty much all of the time, it does make me realise that for a reasonably sane and mild man, I am capable of killing someone! But I do have to reluctantly give them a molecule of respect for the slippery, non-stick way in which they so consistently manage to be so evasive.

What however I do completely take my hat off to them for is their ability to quickly engage people by asking questions and as a direct result create some time and space for themselves. I've noticed that some of them are able to work a room of a hundred people in just over an hour and make everyone in that room that they've met feel like they are the only person that they have met that entire week.

They are able to do this quite simply by asking a few simple questions. Asking questions really is a very useful thing to get back into the habit of doing. Polar Bear Pirates regard question marks as tennis rackets – every time they ask a question, it hits a ball into someone else's court. They refer to them as 'ask rackets'.

When you ask a question it buys you some time whilst the person you've asked has to (a) Think of an answer and (b) Answer it. It also puts you in control because it puts them on the back foot doing all the running. And, if you ask questions about their favourite specialist subject, i.e. them, it makes them feel good and gets them talking, which gives you even more time and space!

Asking questions may not give you all the time in the world but it will buy you some much needed space to enable you to think on your feet. It also has a tendency of helping people to come across as far more knowledgeable on a subject than they actually are!

No matter what team you're leading there are no two bigger things to focus in on than:

(a)   Your people

(b)   Where you as a team are heading

Polar Bear Pirates know that to be effective leaders they must make time to listen and lead. Your people should be the most treasured resource you have and as such you should always be there for them. You have, if you want to show you care, to make time for them and for their sake, get your head up now and again and take a good look at where you're heading and what lies ahead.

'Your people should be the most treasured resource you have and as such you should always be there for them.'

The reason we need to make time for our people is that motivation is like any battery, it needs to be fully connected and constantly charged, otherwise it will go flat. You can't just rev people up and then walk away. They need to be continuously engaged, ener-gised and in some cases loved. Especially the Sleepwalkers, once awake they need to be kept awake otherwise the minute you turn your back, Planet Complacency will decide that it's time they had another little nap and they'll soon be snoozing.

In reality though you only have limited time and unless you have some magic power that the rest of us haven't been lucky enough to acquire as yet, you can't be everywhere for everyone all at the same time. Somehow you have to free up some of your valuable time and delegate responsibility and ownership to the people you've identified as Amps in your team, your corner pieces. Involve them as much as possible, have them feeling fully validated, really humming and sparking everyone up.

So make use of them, give them some challenges that will really test them and allow them the opportunity to release their potential, use their talents and skills. And when I say challenge them, I mean really challenge them. Let them show you, the rest of the team and themselves just what they can do. It's amazing how people when you put your faith in them rise to challenges and, given half a chance astound themselves with what they are capable of.

It is vital that if you don't want to let your people down and you do want to move your team out into the fast lane and keep them out there, that you remain free to lead. Polar Bear Pirates know that leading from the front is extremely important, but they also know that there are times when they need to step back. Not too far back so they lose touch, but far enough back to get things in perspective and get a better view of the road ahead.

You also need to avoid getting drawn in by The Pothole People, particularly when it comes to them trying to suck in as many people as possible into playing their favourite game of crack spotting. It is important that you see and fix the cracks that you and members of your team can fix but don't go falling down the ones that you can't!

The last thing your people who are depending on your support need is for you to start wasting what time you do have or draining your energy banging your head against immovable objects or by getting bogged down with loads of energy absorbing, irrelevant stuff.

A lot of good managers slowly become demotivated because after being in a role for some time they discover that there are certain things that even with their talents and the best will in the world they're never going to change. They lose focus on the big picture and allow all the unimportant things to take over and in some instances, end up becoming completely obsessed with them.

The reality is that no matter how successful it is, if we look long and hard enough at any organisation, large or small, we will eventually see some cracks. At times some are probably even held together behind the scenes by sticky tape and Blu-Tack. But so what! If we as leaders spend our time staring at all the little cracks that we can't do anything about, in our minds, they'll just seem to get bigger and bigger and we'll end up getting nowhere.

One thing to be aware of is that it's not just The Pothole People who go around pointing cracks out. Those who are thinking of leaving and are in the process of selling it to themselves that they're not happy where they are may also be doing a bit of crack spotting and turning a few mole hills into mountains. That's why so many people having left organisations for 'greener grass' often come back.

The key is for all of us to stay focused on the things that really matter and that we can improve. Pothole People, especially the Neg Ferrets tend to focus on the things they can't change, safe in the knowledge that they can bleat on all day about them, knowing full well that they'll never have to get off their whinging butts and do anything about them. For this very reason I've always been amused by people continuously moaning about the weather. Maybe if one day we ever get to control our own weather, they'll shut up moaning about it and just concentrate on everything else they can find wrong with being alive.

One of the biggest mistakes I made early on as a coaching style leader, always relishing a motivational challenge, was wasting time trying to motivate and turn around diehard Pothole People instead of putting my most precious assets, my time and energy into the ninety-eight percent of people who did want to make things happen.

If you are a person who like me loves a challenge, it's easy to concentrate your efforts on turning round Pothole People and their wonderful talent for spotlighting the reasons why not. My attitude to them these days is to put some effort into them but only for a limited amount of time. I set a date in my mind and if after that date it's still a one way street and I can see no change, I just put all my focus back into those who do want to come on the journey.

Hopefully the heat generated by all of us as a team will be enough to eventually burn off their negativity, turn them around and get them onboard pulling with the rest of us. If they do continue to be permanent back seat passengers, non-stop pointing out problems to every solution and pulling the rest of the team down, we'll just have to try and drop them off if we can, along with their bag of grumbles at the next bus stop and fingers crossed, they'll manage to hitch a ride with the competition!

Advise Pothole People not to go around moaning because forty-nine percent of the people they moan to don't care and the other fifty-one percent are glad, glad it's not them.

Your Ground Rules

Being a good leader can at times be a lonely and tough position to be in. Making the right decisions can be hard and it's inevitable that at times you won't be able to please everybody. If you are to be an effective leader you will have to be prepared, to put it bluntly, to 'p' some people off.

In times of emergency when there is no time for discussion you will have to quickly move from being a SONAR leader and become a dictator, telling people what to do. People will look to you in times of crisis for guidance, and you alone are going to have to make some quick and difficult decisions. You are going to have to be brave, very brave!

If you do try and be a miracle worker and achieve the impossible by pleasing all of your people all of the time, you're going to end up as a Big Chum manager, a highly ineffective manager who is skidding further and further down the slippery slope of inconsistency.

A Big Chum manager is someone who wants to be popular, to be everybody's friend. As a result they end up coming across as weak and indecisive, running around all over the place and bending over like a juggling contortionist in an attempt to try and keep all the plates spinning and everybody happy.

If you are to create a high performance culture, as I mentioned earlier, you're going to have to be prepared to screw up and make some wrong decisions. However, provided you make your decisions for all the right reasons, that you own up to your mistakes and are willing to learn from them, your people will support you because as discussed earlier on, they will see you as imperfect but honest.

People are far more likely to follow a strong but human leader who makes the odd mistake rather than someone who pretends not to ever make mistakes or worst still, never makes a mistake because they never make a decision.

So far in this book I have been looking at the importance of developing a caring SONAR leadership style, a coaching, mentoring style that sees the best in people and tries to get it out of them.

Unfortunately there is also a harsher side to being a good leader. There are times when, if we are going to be effective leaders, we will not only have to be brave we will also have to be seen to have teeth.

I know from experience that if you do adopt a caring SONAR leadership style some people in your team, especially Pothole People will mistake this caring side as a soft side, a weakness that could potentially be exploited. As a responsible leader you want to be seen as being fair but believe you me, the last thing you do want to be seen as is being soft. If given the slightest of chances some people will try and walk all over you.

All great leaders you will ever read about will often have been described by their people as 'firm but fair'. That's exactly how I think anyone in leadership should be seen, people like working for people who they know where they stand with them.

'People like working for people who they know where they stand with them.'

To really motivate people, as well as being seen as caring you will need to be seen as being strong. This means being completely upfront and honest with them. It's a good idea to try and have as much clarity around you as possible so everyone knows exactly where they are with you, what they can expect from you and in return what you expect from them. Let people know where your lines are, the things that you find acceptable and the things that you don't.

At the same time it's equally important that you find out what their lines are and for that matter, everyone in the team knows each other's, understands them and respects them. This way everyone gets on a lot better and achieves an awful lot more together.

Whenever I was taking over a new team or new members were joining us, I would explain to them the level of support I was prepared to give them, which was nothing less than five hundred percent, all of the time. I would make a commitment to them then and there to give them this along with all my help, knowledge, time and energy to really make things work.

I would then draw a rectangle on a board or a flip chart and draw around the edges of it the following words, Honesty: Timekeeping:

Mistakes?: Help? And in the middle of the rectangle I would draw a big smile and write the words Let Your Face Know!

In an open and frank way I would then explain to them that these are my personal ground rules, my lines. They are:

- That I need everyone to always be honest with me, I can't stand being fed the bovine stuff.

- I expect people to always be on time for me because I'm a bit of a stickler for punctuality, if people are continually late, I begin to assume that they don't really care anymore.

- When they make a mistake, to put their hand up and the attitude of myself and all my team will be 'No problem, what do we do to correct it?'

- If anyone needs help to ask for it rather than getting out of their depth.

- And finally, if they are enjoying themselves to let their face know!

In return for my total commitment to them I would then ask them to give me their commitment to these five things. Some of you reading this may think than I'm sounding like I'm trying to come across as some sort of hard ball Sergeant Shout, well I'm most certainly not. I'm merely trying to make life a lot simpler for everyone by being completely upfront and transparent about my expectations, likes and dislikes and, hopefully in doing so, greatly improve our chances as a team of reaching Fat City.

As well as this, what in effect I am also doing is drawing the shape of my integrity as a leader. I want all my people to have a clearly defined picture of what I'm all about and the values I stand for. I also deliberately want everyone to know that as well as being a compassionate leader, that if people do deliberately cross my boundaries and stray beyond 'Happy Valley', I will bite.

No matter whatever else they may say about me in bars after work, I would be chuffed to bits and know that I am doing my job well if my people when they do talk about me say things like 'He's a good boss to work for, he's dedicated, caring, passionate and a lot of fun, but don't ever try giving him any bull or turn up late for one of his meetings, it's not a pleasant experience!'

If you were taking over a new team right now, what would your ground rules be, what are your expectations, your lines? What does the shape of your integrity look like?

The Power of Peers

Use the power of peers to motivate and also keep your team focused. There is no more powerful form of recognition or motivational pressure than that which comes from people's own team mates. You don't want to have to spend your time keeping people in line and you most certainly don't want to become seen as the team's resident police officer.

The power of peers has such a powerful influence on all of us because it's a deep rooted tribal thing that goes back a very long way. The need for all of us to belong to and be accepted by our peer group that we have found ourselves relating to and identifying with, is at our very core as human beings. It's part of our genetic makeup, it's in our DNA.

Being made to feel very much part of our group, having some standing within it, gaining recognition and respect from its members, is for the vast majority of people, a very warm feeling. On the other side of the coin, suddenly finding ourselves on the outside of that group usually gives us a very cold feeling of isolation, something that we as humans are not very good at handling.

As a result of wanting to stay within our group, be recognised and accepted and, at the same time, not wanting to let those around us down that we care about and respect, those little widgets once again spring into action.

I will never ever forget the awful feeling I had when I first ever experienced the lasting effects of the power of peer pressure when, as a young policeman, I let down my beloved team – Group 2 Alpha Tango. My widget was truly detonated on that day, big time. I had pulled a sickie and in doing so I had left my already desperately under resourced team even more short staffed. On the evening of the day I was supposedly off sick with a stomach bug I had been spotted enjoying a meal with some friends in a restaurant. When I next turned up for duty the boisterous locker room fell silent and a friend of mine told me that 'Twiggy' (Inspector Allen) wanted to see me.

I had experienced a few good dressing downs in life, but none of them would have anything like the lasting effect that the one 'Twiggy' Allen was about to give me. I was just about to experience what today I describe as the most motivational rollocking of my life.

He didn't raise his voice, he didn't swear and he didn't verbally attack me. He spoke softly and quietly as he read through a list of incidents that had happened in the St Pauls area whilst I'd been enjoying my unauthorised day off, one of which was particularly harrowing and deeply upsetting. He then addressed the task that I hadn't performed and went on to remind me of the one word that bonded us all together as a team, trust.

I will never forget the feeling I had of letting myself, my team mates and 'Twiggy' down so badly and of wanting so desperately to try and make it up to them. I never did it again and I still regret it to this day.

A very popular peer recognition idea that really does get people motivated is Pit Stops. The idea for them came from my wife Louise telling me that because weekends for us as a family often get so busy, she wished that now and again she could have a couple of hours off work during the week, just to catch up with a few things.

A Pit Stop is an hour off work. At the end of each day everyone in a team gets together for a huddle meet. I used to have them at the beginning and at the end of each day to help keep my teams pumped up and focused. They are very brief 'gather round' meetings that last no more than two minutes. During the end of day huddle meets, non management staff vote in their teams to award Pit Stops to members of their team whom they feel have really taken that extra step. Please note, they are not handed out like sweets; on some days several may be awarded and on other days none at all.

Team members save up their Pit Stops and use them for when they need to take time off work. I know most companies limit them so people can only take a maximum of say up to four hours off at any one time.

Through peer recognition you are highlighting success and rewarding people with time for being productive in your time. They really do work. People go like cats on kippers to win them.

Get out of That Box!

L ike me you probably hear a lot of managers talking about thinking outside the box and yet they sit inside the same old box trying to come up with new, out of the box ideas.

Often a lack of walls, a change of scenery, no ceilings, a different environment and being able to step back with some fresh air going up a team's nostrils really does induce corkscrew thinking. And, if you really want to help them come up with some stonking ideas, hold your brain storm meetings by the side of water.

Noisy water is the ultimate, especially when it's going over a waterfall, through an old water wheel or crashing up on a beach but it doesn't really matter too much if you don't have any noisy water near you. Try going for a walk along a river bank, a canal, hire a boat, sit on a beach, by a lake, a reservoir, loch or even a big pond, so long as it's outside and it's by water!

Water seems to relax and sooth people, helping them to gain access to the hard drive areas of their minds where all their creative pictures are generated.

Another enjoyable experience that always seems to aid people with accessing their hard drives is cooking and eating outdoors. If you are going to give it a try, everyone has to be involved in the preparation and the cooking side, and not just the eating! It's a lot of fun, it's great for team building and food for some reason just seems to taste so much better when cooked outside.

If you can combine enjoying a few gastronomic delights with being alongside water, and perhaps a fun activity of some sort, well then you've got the ultimate out of box, brain storm meeting experience, and that's bound to be a winner.

A few of the 'What No Walls' ideas that people have come up with in my workshops:

- Canal Boat Meetings

- Soup Tasting Session

- Cliff Path Walk

- Conker Competition

- River Bank Picnic

- Back Woods Cook Ups
- Stone Skimming Competition
- Beach BBQ
- Bacon, Sausage & Veggie Option Sandwich Meets
- Marshmallow Toasting
- Inspirational Landmark Meets (e.g. On The London Eye)
- Bonfire Building
- Horse Chestnut Roasting
- Tea Tasting
- Tree Planting
- Jacket Potato Fest
- An Outdoor Bake Off
- Pancake Tossing
- Kite Flying

The key is to keep it fun, when people start laughing and coming up with outrageous ideas, that's when you'll know its working because that's when their minds and not just their bodies are now well and truly outside their box.

Just let things roll and I guarantee it won't be too long before someone says 'Actually that isn't such a daft idea, but what we could do is . . . !' It's another oldie but another firm favourite of Polar Bear Pirates – 'The only daft idea is the idea you keep to yourself'.

If possible it's helpful if people don't bring their mobile phones with them, but you have just one in case of an emergency or for urgent calls from the office. The fewer interruptions the better, it works best if people are able to fully immerse themselves in what you're discussing. And, if you're not going to go for a culinary option, make sure you still take along a few snacks!

If only just for an hour or so, as well as assisting innovative thinking, getting out of that box now and then is great for team bonding. It helps empower individuals and it also makes a very welcome change for them. Even if you don't come up with a whole bunch of stunning new ideas, everyone will still come back feeling refreshed, hopefully having enjoyed some great food and having had an opportunity to have a real input. As one big sharing team, you'll have taken another step forward together.

If for some reason it's not possible to hold your meeting outside, go to another indoor venue that has a completely different feel to it than the one that you usually use. If you can have some food together there, again something that's a bit different from what people normally have, that will help. And, if health and safety permits, if you want to create a really good atmosphere to entice some original thinking, darken a room and light a few candles around the place!

The Dent You Leave Behind

A final thought. Never under estimate for one moment the impact that you have on others. You'll probably be quite astonished by the dent that you as an individual can make in people's minds.

After all these years of living with yourself you've probably got fairly used to being you. As a result of knowing all your own personal little habits and foibles you may not at times, especially when you're not feeling on top form, think that you could have a particularly big influence on others. If this should ever be the case, you will not be far more wrong. As a leader you should never underestimate the impact that you have on people around you, people who haven't had the chance to get to know you as well as you do, especially new starters in your team.

'As a leader you should never underestimate the impact that you have on people around you.'

The reason your impact is often bigger than you think it is, is quite simply because the image that people see is usually considerably bigger than the person behind it. People's images in the workplace are like objects under water, they look bigger than what they actually are and are not always where they appear to be.

As well as appearing bigger, people never quite see you as you think they do. The image that you think you portray, even if you have a really good long look at yourself in a mirror and occasionally catch a rare glimpse of the back of yourself, isn't the image that others see. Good news for some of us!

Have you ever heard a recording of your own voice? It doesn't sound like you, does it?! Which, if you think about it is absurd, seeing as your ears are only a few centimetres away from your mouth.

Your ability to inspire people will be determined to a large extent by their perceptions of you. These varying perceptions will take the form of a series of pictures in their minds, created mainly through TNT snapshots.

You'll never have complete ownership over your own image because people will take away whatever pictures they want to but you can certainly have a lot of control, most of the time. People might not always see where you're coming from, what you think you're giving out might not be what they're seeing. In other words, at first they won't always get you.

My very first impression of 'Twiggy' Allen was that of a reserved person who appeared a bit standoffish, slightly aloof even. How wrong I was! I realised as I got to know him that I'd just happened to have come across him in one of his quieter, reflective, taking-it-all in moods. As a SONAR leader he'd been standing back, listening and absorbing.

I know over the years that as a leader, I've been read wrong on many an occasion. It's actually very frustrating when you're passionate about something, trying to do what's best for everyone and you're doing all you can to be open with people and engage with them, but at the same time you realise that some people just aren't 'getting' you and in some cases you sense that maybe they don't really trust you.

Now and again after one of my presentations I'll get someone come up to me and tell me that to start with, they weren't quite sure about me! If you are going to dare to be innovative and do things differently, not everyone is going to buy into you straight away. You can't expect to instantly win everyone over overnight. **Engagement isn't an instant thing, it doesn't come in a tin.**

People need time to adjust to change and some will take longer than others to adapt to new ways of thinking and to getting used to you. But, if you're always yourself, completely honest with them, passionate about what you do and you're doing everything you possibly can to try and get on their wave length, they will eventually see the real you.

When trying to engage Sleepwalkers this is something you should be aware of. With some of them, you're going to have to be prepared to really stick at it, to be patient, to have a lot of faith and belief in yourself and even more in them.

Be you, have fun, keep on caring and be careful of that image of yours, you never know where it's next going to leave behind a very big dent or who it's going to wake!

When giving a presentation don't try and deliver too many messages. Those in the audience will take away a maximum of three, and months later may remember just one. If you were to lie down on a bed of a thousand six inch nails it would feel very uncomfortable for you. If however you were to take away nine hundred and ninety nine nails and leave just one, and then lie down on that, it would crucify you! That's what happens when you try and get across lots of messages all at once, you

blunt the key message you want to deliver. Stick with just a couple – Far more effective.

This I know sounds like obvious advice but you'd be amazed by the number of intelligent people who I see at conferences blowing their opportunity of delivering an impactful message by overcrowding their presentation.

Health Warning

F ear was originally established in all of us for a very good reason, to protect us from doing things like walking off cliffs or wandering up to venomous snakes in the wild and patting them on the head. Fear in itself is not an enemy, it is there to look after us.

However as humans we are prone to worrying about things that haven't happened yet, that we have no prior experience of and that are unlikely to happen to us, things that are purely figments of our own imagination.

One of man's oldest enemies, The Worry Worm is a particular virulent virus which was well documented by The Romans and described by them as 'eating away at you'. This performance damaging virus uses your unfounded fears to bury its way into the picture files of the hard drive of your mind, where it hides in the guise of being a friend, pretending only to want to take care of you.

When a big, important event in your life is coming up, it gets busy feeding on your very worst possible nightmare pictures, conjuring up fictitious pictures of potential disasters in your imagination and exaggerating and distorting out of all proportion any past minor failures.

If not controlled it could become a serious health risk and hold you back from achieving your goals for the rest of your life. Allowed to run free it will simply grow bigger and bigger, slowly burrowing deeper, corrupting more and more of your picture files. As it takes up more space on your hard drive, it will gradually take up more of your time, sapping your self-belief, eating away your confidence and draining you of all your energy.

Its favourite food is the odd juicy negative passing comment made to you by other people. If you take to heart the poison comments of The Pothole People you will merely be feeding this all consuming virus.

You will never ever be able to completely eradicate it, everyone worries about things that they shouldn't we wouldn't be human if we didn't. But, you can minimise and contain it simply by not feeding it. Don't feed your worry worm by dwelling on the negative opinions of others or by concentrating on the downside pictures. The more you look at them the fatter your worry worm will become. It will only begin to diminish in size if you stay focused on the positive pictures and keeping yourself and fellow travellers firmly on course to reach Fat City.

'Don't feed your worry worm by dwelling on the negative opinions of others or by concentrating on the downside pictures.'

Six Polar Bear Pirate Attitudes for The Journey Ahead

For more info please visit www.adrianwebster.com

Polar Bear Pirate Terminology

44.4: Your time on this planet
Amps: Those who give off energy
Ask Rackets: Questions designed to put the ball in other's courts

BC: Before Conditioning
BEDS: Big Exciting Dreams
Belief Thermals: Soaring up and down levels of belief
Betty Backroom: The unsung heroine of any great team who gets things done and manages her boss
Big Chum Manager: A manager who wants to be everyone's friend
Big E's: Endorphines
BLOATERS: Boasting Lazy Obnoxious And Tediously Egotistical Reptilian Saddos
Bubble Wrapping: Popping SMUGS along the road to Fat City
Bunker Brain: An entrenched mind that is impregnable to new ideas

Cartoon Attitude: The childlike attitude of Polar Bear Pirates
Corkscrew Thinking: Around walls thinking

DIY Belief: Do It Yourself belief
Dolly Team: A whole team of clones
DOT Team: A spot on, focused team benefiting from Diversity Of Thought
Dunking: The art of dipping in and out of the hard drive of the mind to snatch good ideas

Egg In Fridge: A real burning deep down need

FAFF Time: Family And Friends First time
Fat City: Where the winners live
Fat City Road Map: A map of alternative routes to Fat City
Four B's: The four most likely places to have a good idea: Bed, Bog, Bath or Bar

The Gap: The small but perilous area between planning and doing

Happy Valley: Where everyone gets on well with their neighbours
Head Treads: The ladder pullers of Fat City
Heat Seeking Neg Ferret: A particularly determined Neg Ferret
Herd Heads: Followers of popular opinion
Hissy Pissy Pythons: People working in customer facing roles who don't like customers
Hitchers: Passengers in teams looking for free rides
Hummers: Those who give out so much energy they hum

I'm Just: A person with low self esteem

Jaffa Gaffa: A manager who is a cake amongst biscuits- they think they are better than everyone else

Looking Between Your Legs: Seeing the world through the eyes of a child

LUST Relationships: Relationships based on Loyalty Understanding Sharing and Trust

Mind Modem: Modulates and demodulates speech into 3D pictures
Molasses Man: A sweet but slow person burdened by the beliefs of others

Neg Ferrets: Seekers of negativity
Neg Fraternity: The brotherhood of Pothole People
Noddy's: Brief and creative moments when we slip into our open hard drive area
Norms: Average pedestrian people
N'T's: Negative words used by Sinkers to implant sinking thinking

One Degree Club: A group of extraordinary people who take that extra step

Pants Porters: Those who bring their old team's bad habits with them
PBPs: Polar Bear Pirates
PHPs: Proactively Helpful People
Picture Box Files: Where people's 3D pictures of past experiences are saved
Pineapple People: Scary looking people who are actually very sweet
Pit Stops: Collectable periods of time off work awarded as peer recognition

Planet Complacency: The arch enemy of success
Point Plonk: The precise moment beyond which there is no return when dunking
POP: Power Of Picture
Pothole People: Enemies along the road to Fat City
Prisoners of POO: Those held back by People's Old Opinions
Pumpkin People: Unnoticed for 364 days of the year until they light up with their annual bright idea

Quitter: Where the Nobody's live

RC'd: Reconditioned
Rock Bottom: Where most winners come from

Sand Writers: Those who leave behind their mark
Sergeant Shout: A manager who tries to rule by fear
Self Lickers: Those who worship at their own shrine
Sinkers: Fat City dropouts trying to sink other people's attempts at reaching it
Sinking Thinking: Negative thinking put into people's heads by Sinkers
Sleepwalkers: 'Guests' of Planet Complacency
SMUGS: Small Unseen Goals
Snapshots: Memorable TNT images of people
Snigger Trigger Tags: Amusing, devious label tags used to quickly locate picture files
SONAR: Sounding Out Needs And Responding
Stop Bombs: No entry judgments dropped on talented people by Head Treads

Surfs Up: When everything is just rocking along

Time Con: A Polar Bear Pirate con used in an attempt to
speed time up when doing crummy jobs
Ticking Team: A successful team that's working well
TNTs: Tiny Noticeable Things
TOES: Tag On Extensions that people add on to their answers

Ugly Butter: Malicious gossip

Vamps: Those who need to feed off the energy of others

Widgets of Fear: In mind detonators of positive pressure to
help boost performance

Worry Worm: A virus that feeds on fear and saps self belief

XY's: Unknown people who didn't believe in themselves or life
before death

Y Fronts: People who are all front, giving it the big 'Yes' but
never deliver because they're just pants

Zoo Team: A talented team of free minded but restricted
individuals

About Adrian Webster

Milkman, policeman and salesman were just a few of the entries on Adrian's CV before he moved into the IT industry and discovered an extraordinary ability to engage and inspire others to achieve success. The son of a Yorkshire coal miner, he is now a bestselling business author and one of the most popular motivational speakers in Europe today.

For more information regarding Adrian's speaking or his workshops, please visit www.adrianwebster.com

Lightning Source UK Ltd.
Milton Keynes UK
UKOW06f1150160816

280810UK00005B/15/P